Mary: "It won't be long until we begin at the academy

Katarina: "Y-Yeah, I guess..." (But only Catastrophic

Sophia: "Yes... It is quite exciting indeed."

> Katarina is about to embark on a new adventure...

Eheheheh. How exciting."
Bad Ends await me there!)

FORTUNE·LOVER

My Next Life as a VILLAINESS: ALL ROUTES LEAD TO DOOM!

VOLUME 2

SATORU YAMAGUCHI
ILLUSTRATIONS BY NAMI HIDAKA

My Next Life as a Villainess: All Routes Lead to Doom! Volume 2
by Satoru Yamaguchi

Translated by Shirley Yeung
Edited by Aimee Zink

Copyright © 2015 Satoru Yamaguchi
Illustrations by Nami Hidaka

First published in Japan in 2015 by Ichijinsha Inc., Tokyo.
Publication rights for this English edition arranged through Kodansha Ltd., Tokyo.

Find more books like this one at www.j-novel.club!

President and Publisher: Samuel Pinansky
Managing Editor: Aimee Zink

ISBN: 978-1-7183-6661-9
Printed in Korea
First Printing: July 2020
10 9 8 7 6 5 4 3 2 1

Contents

My Next Life All Routes

Jeord Stuart

The third prince of the kingdom, and Katarina's fiancé. Although he looks like a fairy-tale prince with his blonde hair and blue eyes, he secretly harbors a twisted and terrible nature. He once spent his days in boredom, never showing interest in anything, until he met Katarina Claes. His magical element is Fire.

Katarina Claes

The only daughter of Duke Claes. Has slanted ey and angled features, which she thinks make her lo like a villainess. After her memories of her past l returned, she transformed from a spoiled noble la to a problem child. Although she often gets ahe of herself, she is an honest and straightforward gi She has below-average academic and magic ability. Her magical element is Earth.

Young Katarina

as a Villainess: Lead to Doom!

Nicol Ascart

The son of Royal Chancellor Ascart. An incredibly beautiful and alluring young man who loves his sister, Sophia, deeply. His magical element is Wind.

Keith Claes

Katarina's adopted brother, taken in by the Claes family due to his magical aptitude. Considerably handsome, and seen by others as a chivalrous ladies' man. His magical element is Earth.

Alan Stuart

Jeord's twin brother, and the fourth prince of the kingdom. Wildly handsome but also surly and arrogant. Often compares himself to his genius brother, and sulks when he realizes he can't catch up. His magical element is Water.

Sophia Ascart

Daughter of Royal Chancellor Ascart, and Nicol's younger sister. Used to face discrimination due to her white hair and red eyes. A calm and peaceful girl.

Mary Hunt

Fourth daughter of Marquis Hunt, and Alan's fiancée. A lovely and charming girl who's well known as the perfect image of a noble lady.

Maria Campbell

A commoner, but also a rare "Wielder of Light." The original protagonist of *Fortune Lover* who is very hardworking and loves baking.

Sirius Dieke

The only child of Marquess Dieke. The calm and sweet president of the student council. Ranked top of his class in both academics and magical studies.

Milidiana Claes

Katarina's mother, and wife of Duke Claes. Has angled features like her daughter.

Luigi Claes

Katarina's father, a Duke and head of the Claes family. Spoils his daughter.

Anne Shelley

Katarina's personal maid who has been with her since childhood.

I am Katarina Claes, daughter of Duke Claes and heir to the Claes family. When I was eight years old, I hit my head on a rock and suddenly realized that I had been reborn into the world of *Fortune Lover*, the otome game that I was playing before my untimely death.

In fact, I happen to be the main antagonist of the game. Katarina Claes is supposed to be a villainous noble lady who gets in the protagonist's way and bullies her. At the end of the game, her fate is to either be exiled from the kingdom or meet a gruesome end at the hands of the protagonist's love interest — nothing but bad endings!

Naturally I don't want to get killed! But getting exiled from the kingdom wouldn't leave me with much chance of survival either. It's so unfair! After my early death in my previous life, I want to live to a ripe old age this time, spending my golden years with a cat on my lap as I elegantly bask in the sun! I don't want to be involved in these social politics of love and intrigue, much less get killed by them! No matter what, I am determined to overcome these Catastrophic Bad Ends and live a long, peaceful life!

First, I had to deal with one of the guys who could bring Katarina Claes to a Bad End — her fiancé Jeord, the third prince.

In *Fortune Lover*, Katarina, who had been bullying the protagonist all along, would either be exiled by him or die by his blade in retaliation for attacking the protagonist. So I've made some plans in case those things happen. If I get exiled, I'll use my magical abilities to earn a living. From what I remember, magical aptitude is rare outside of my kingdom. Or if Jeord comes at me with a sword, I'll use my highly realistic projectile snake to terrorize him, since he hates snakes. Then I'd use that opening to dodge his attacks.

And so I've tried my best to improve my magic, while at the same time constantly refining the appearance of my projectile snakes with the help of the head gardener, Grandpa Tom. I've also started taking my swordplay training more seriously, so I can hold my own if I'm ever attacked.

Another person I have to deal with is Katarina's adopted brother, Keith Claes. He could also bring a Catastrophic Bad End down on me. In his route, Katarina bullies the protagonist terribly as usual, and Keith retaliates by either exiling or killing his sister with his powerful magic. To be fair, Katarina is so horrible that she leaves a deep scar on the protagonist in that scenario.

In order to head these endings off, I made sure that Keith was never lonely. I kept him company, inviting him out to play every day. In *Fortune Lover*, he lives an isolated and alienated life until he is healed by the protagonist's gentle nature, and he naturally falls in love with her.

All I have to do is ensure that Keith is never lonely — simple as that! He'll never fall for the protagonist in the first place. With those thoughts in mind, I took him with me everywhere I went within the manor, and eventually outside its walls too.

I worked really hard these past seven years. Everything had to be done before I began attending the Academy of Magic! Luckily, my efforts paid off. By my fifteenth birthday I was being praised for my skill at the sword, and my projectile snakes looked just like the real thing. And Keith had been raised lovingly, and was no longer lonely or sad. Well done, me!

Unfortunately, one thing didn't turn out like I'd planned: my magical ability. I thought that if I buried my head in magical studies and practiced enough that I could make a living if I were exiled from the kingdom, but it just didn't work. No matter how hard I tried, my magical powers didn't increase. I couldn't cast a single spell other than "Dirt Bump." That spell would be useless for making a living, so I had to change my plans. Right now, I'm practicing growing plants and tilling the earth so I might be able to live as a farmer.

With all this in place due to seven years' worth of hard work, the countermeasures to the Catastrophic Bad Ends are now complete. It will soon be time for me to go to the Academy of Magic.

Slowly but surely, the white breath of winter was drawing to an end. The gardens of Claes Manor, already feeling the warm embrace of spring, were filled with crop fields — my work over the past seven years, of course.

I would start my school life at the Academy of Magic's dormitories soon, so I'd have to say goodbye to my fields for a while. I felt kind of lonely looking out at the familiar rows of crops.

"We will go to the Academy of Magic soon. Very soon indeed, eheheh. I do look forward to it," Mary Hunt said, her usual lovely smile flitting across her beautiful features. In *Fortune Lover*, Mary was a rival character just like Katarina.

"Y-Yeah… I guess…" To me, setting foot into an academy where I'd probably meet my doom was no laughing matter — but of course, I couldn't say something like that to the gently smiling Mary.

"I am really… looking forward to it, too…" Sophia Ascart said with a smile. She was yet another rival character in the original game.

"Y-Yeah… Of course." Surrounded by those eager smiles, I couldn't just go and tell them that I was terrified at the idea.

These two people never had any contact with Katarina Claes in the events of *Fortune Lover*. If anything, they disliked her for her villainous ways. But Mary and Sophia were now my close friends, having visited me in my manor regularly for the past seven years.

"And what exactly is it that you're all so enraptured by?" A familiar voice, and an equally familiar suspicious smile — the voice belonged to none other than Jeord Stuart, third prince of the kingdom, and my fiancé.

Originally, Jeord was pretty uninterested in Katarina and hardly had any interactions with her. But for some reason he had started visiting me at my manor for days at a time, and now was another close friend of mine.

"Ah, Prince Jeord. We were just talking of the anticipation we felt towards our beginning at the academy."

"Ah, I see. Of course, it is worth looking forward to indeed," Jeord responded with a seemingly genuine smile on his face.

Hmm. Apparently even Jeord is looking forward to this…

As for me, I wasn't looking forward to this whole academy thing at all. Thinking about the story of *Fortune Lover* made me depressed, for one thing. After all, it was the place where all those Catastrophic Bad Ends were waiting for me! But besides that, it was a school for magical studies, so it would be a lot of work for me. I really couldn't get excited about academy life. Why was everyone so fired up about this whole thing?

"Umm… how come all of you are so eager to go to the academy…?" I asked my overenthusiastic friends.

"But of course, because I can spend all that time together with you, Lady Katarina...!" Mary said. She was visibly excited, her cheeks a healthy shade of crimson.

"Yes...! Exactly! We'll be able to spend all that time together... with Lady Katarina, once we go!" Sophia declared, her expression strangely similar to Mary's.

Now that they mention it, I guess they do have a point. Being so preoccupied with the Bad Ends, I had forgotten about the happy days that I'd spend at the academy with my dear friends. Thinking about things that way, the academy wouldn't be so bad after all.

"I am sure that we will be in the same dormitory, Katarina. Do feel free to visit me in my room. For you, I will prepare special snacks and sweets," Jeord said with a charming smile.

Ooh, special snacks and sweets prepared by a prince! I'm definitely interested in that...

"Yes! I would love to—"

"But you mustn't, Big Sister! Living spaces in the dormitories are segregated by gender! You must never do such a thing...!" Keith said, suddenly coming between Jeord and me, looking flustered.

Although the Keith from the game hated Katarina and did his best to avoid her, he had long since grown attached to me — probably because I dragged him around with me so much. Now, he was the perfect little brother, always looking out for his sister.

"Keith, you are correct to a certain degree. While it is true that living spaces are segregated by gender, visiting another's room is hardly an issue as long as permission is acquired beforehand."

"That is *if* it is acquired! Relatives would be one thing, but Big Sister entering the room of a man, and a *stranger*, would be out of the question."

11

"What is all this talk of strangers about? I am engaged to Katarina, if you recall — hardly a stranger, wouldn't you say? What about you, Keith Claes? Are you not merely her adopted brother?"

"At the moment you are nothing more than her fiancé, Prince Jeord. Should the engagement ever be canceled, she and you would be nothing but strangers."

"Ah, but do you think I would ever cancel the engagement?"

And there they went again — Keith and Jeord having their own happy conversation with faces full of smiles. Considering that these two hardly ever spoke to each other in the original game, I was surprised by how they were now steadfast friends. In fact, they left me out of their fun private conversations all the time.

Given how well my brother got along with Jeord, it would be a tragedy if they both ended up falling for the protagonist at the academy. *Ah, it would be so sad if one girl divided such a close pair of friends! I hope they find some other wonderful girls, as long as they aren't the protagonist.*

"...But yes... there would be such dangers in a dormitory setting... we have to think of some sort of countermeasure as well..."

"Hmm? What is it, Mary?" I asked, noticing her murmuring. While my attention had been sidetracked by Jeord and Keith's intense discussion, Mary's expression had turned dark. She seemed to be thinking some very severe thoughts.

"Ah, it is nothing, Lady Katarina... just some things on my mind... But yes, of course! Master Nicol, would you happen to know the general floor plan of the academy's dormitory?"

The one Mary had called out to was Sophia's brother, Nicol Ascart. If we had followed the game's script, we would have never crossed paths at all. He was one of the protagonist's potential romance interests and never had a single meeting with Katarina Claes.

Nicol, however, had ended up becoming one of my good friends too. Being a year older than the rest of us, he had already been at the academy for a year and was currently visiting Claes Manor during his spring break.

Mary's sudden question didn't faze him. Nicol delivered a cool, collected answer with his usual lack of expression. "To a certain extent."

"That should suffice — may I trouble you to enlighten me on the matter? We must take the necessary precautions so that the enemy doesn't do anything untoward during our stay...!" Mary said.

"...I understand."

"Lady Mary, Big Brother, do allow me to assist as well!"

Mary, Nicol, and Sophia called for the servants to bring them pens and paper, before setting it all down on a garden table next to the fields. Then they promptly sat down and started having some kind of serious discussion.

"Hmm...? What are Mary and the rest doing all the way over there...?" I turned to the only person left next to me, who was standing dumbfounded on the spot just like me.

"You're asking me, now? I've got no idea at all," Alan Stuart said, shrugging. He was Jeord's twin, and the fourth prince of the kingdom.

I shouldn't have had anything to do with Alan according to the game, but for one reason or another, he had also become one of my good friends. His response to my question was pretty typical. "I know, right?" I said, gazing at him warmly.

The Alan I knew was straightforward and childlike, and he was pretty dense when it came to noticing what was going on. He was like this in the game too — a childish prince who never realized his own feelings towards the protagonist. *If I can't figure it out, there's no way Alan could.*

"What's with that look?" Alan said, looking surprised. Did he feel like I was making fun of him?

"Ah, it's nothing, Prince Alan. It's just… you're fifteen years of age now… Wouldn't it be best to act a little more like an adult…?" If Alan remained childish and block-headed forever, he would never be able to capture Mary's heart. That was why I offered him my advice.

"…Look who's talking. I'd throw those words right back at your face." This was his rude response. *This is why people think you're childish, Alan!*

I, on the other hand, graciously responded to him. "Ah, how silly of you, Prince Alan. Whatever do you mean? I am quite the noble lady, don't you know?"

He started mumbling something like "Eh? But you're definitely more…" But being the adult I am, I elegantly let it slip by. Meanwhile, Jeord and Keith's intense conversation continued, while Mary and the Ascarts stayed immersed in their serious discussion.

While I still felt kind of uneasy about starting life in this Catastrophic Bad End Academy, the fact that I'd be able to spend time with all my friends was a relief — and a little bit of excitement bloomed in my heart.

If possible, I want to overcome the otome game hell that may lie before me, and then look forward to peaceful days with my dear friends.

My name is Atsuko Sasaki. As of this year, I am thirteen years old. I just started at the local middle school a few days ago... and ended up in the last seat at the back of the classroom. Since then, I've spent my days alone. I just don't feel like I belong here.

I'm surrounded by girls who came from other grade schools, and they've all formed new cliques. I want to have a nice group of friends to spend time with, too... but it seems that I'm not very good at that sort of thing. I don't know how to speak to my classmates... or how to try to be friends with them. I don't understand things like that.

It was the same in grade school — I didn't know how to interact with people, and before I knew it, I was all alone. The other girls saw me as weird and often ignored me. Sometimes they would bully me, or even hide my things... As this went on, I eventually realized that I had become afraid of people. I started keeping to myself, never speaking to anyone around me.

And so... even though middle school is a new place and a new beginning, I can't bring myself to speak to anyone... or even say hello. And so, I've shifted my gaze from the classmates around me who all seem to be enjoying themselves. Instead, I read the books that I brought from home.

These are my favorite books — manga and light novels. If I imagine myself slipping into these stories as I read them, I can forget all about my loneliness. I pretend that I'm the protagonist of these stories. That way, even someone who is lonely, shy, and unhappy like me can become a popular girl who everyone loves.

Today, like usual, I opened my book on my desk. To escape the loneliness of reality...

And so the days went on, and a few weeks passed since I started middle school. After the last homeroom period of the day ended, I walked towards the library to borrow some books. This had been my daily routine for the past few weeks.

After changing out of my indoor shoes, I walked out into the schoolyard. I shot a sideways glance at the athletics club, whose members were doing some sort of practice.

I didn't join any clubs. Honestly, I might have made a friend or two if I had... but I didn't have the courage to simply show up, all by myself, at someone else's club room.

How nice it must be... they look like they're having so much fun, I thought, looking at the girls doing their athletics practice, chatting and laughing. It was then that... it happened.

"Aaaaahhhhh!!!"

I heard a strange sound coming from above, but before I could even look up to check what it was, I heard a loud thud — and felt something hitting me really hard.

I felt my consciousness quickly slipping away.

"Uuuuugghh! I'm really, really sorry...!"

Someone was... crying. I could hear someone crying. Slowly, I opened my eyes... only to see the face of a young girl before me, snot and tears running trails down her face. She seemed to be the one who I'd heard crying.

"AH! She's awake! Nurse! She's awake!!" The girl that I was looking at yelled before dashing away, leaving some white curtains fluttering behind her.

I... don't understand. Was I... asleep? Slowly, I looked at my surroundings. A white ceiling, the swaying white curtains... and then me, lying down on a white bed. While I didn't know where

I was, this ceiling looked familiar — it was exactly like the one in my classroom. If I had to guess, I was still somewhere on the school grounds...

Wha...? But I thought I was heading to the school gates by cutting through the schoolyard... As I was still confused by my thoughts, a woman dressed in white appeared.

"How do you feel? Do you feel dizzy? Do you feel pain anywhere?" the woman asked.

I slowly gave myself a once-over. It didn't really hurt very much anywhere, and my head felt fine. "I... I think I'm okay..."

Upon hearing my answer, the woman in white smiled calmly. "I see. That's great news. However, I still think it would be best for you to get checked up at a hospital just in case there are any complications... I contacted your family a few moments ago."

"...Huh? Hospital? Check-up...?" I couldn't figure out what was happening. I stared at the woman in a daze. The woman seemed to be troubled too, judging by the change in her expression.

"Yes... I suppose this is all very sudden for you. This is the nurse's office — you were brought here after you lost consciousness."

"I... lost? Consciousness?"

Is this the nurse's office? This is the first time I've actually been inside... that's why I didn't know where I was. Then... that woman in white is probably the school nurse.

But... why am I here? I don't have any illnesses, and I don't remember feeling bad today... Then why did I pass out...? More and more questions started to cloud my mind.

As if noticing this, the school nurse smiled at me, although she looked strained this time. "It wasn't because of illness. The reason for you being here is this girl here."

Saying so, the nurse pointed casually at the girl from before, who was now standing by her side. Tears and snot still streaked her face.

"I'm sorry..." the girl said, bowing deeply in my direction. "I just *had* to climb that lovely tree in the schoolyard... I couldn't help myself. I was climbing just fine at first, but then I got too excited and my feet slipped... That's why I fell on you. I'm really sorry..."

Come to think of it, I heard something strange... a voice, maybe? It came from right above me, right before the impact. So that was... this girl falling on me.

But... grade-schoolers might climb trees, but a middle-schooler? And at school, too...? I didn't understand what the girl was talking about — especially the part about "that lovely tree."

I took a closer look at the girl. She was still hanging her head as she kept apologizing profusely. She was wearing our school's uniform, but her skirt was caked with dirt and wrinkled. She must have gotten it dirty when she fell from the tree... but did that mean she was climbing in her skirt? At school...? She really was a strange girl

"Um... it's alright, really..." I couldn't stand seeing this girl repeatedly apologizing and bowing to me.

"...But!" The girl still seemed distraught, so I repeated myself.

"It... really is okay. Please don't worry about it."

This was the very same girl who had landed on top of me, falling from above without warning. Maybe I should have been angry at her. But she was apologizing so much and looked like she really felt bad. For some reason, I couldn't dislike this girl if I tried. There was just something about her, with her flustered face and furrowed brows.

"It was an accident... Please, it's alright. More importantly... are you injured? After falling like that...?"

At those words, the girl smiled widely. "I'm fine! Thank you, Sasaki-san. You're really kind." The girl, who had been crying up until now, was now grinning.

But… "Why do you know my name?" *How could she know that? Did she look through my belongings, maybe?*

"What do you mean? Of course I know your name, we're in the same class!"

"Wha?!" I stared intently at the girl's surprised expression. *Come to think of it… it really does seem like I've seen her somewhere before.*

Oh, right… we're classmates. I had been reading books on my own for these past weeks since starting middle school, so I hardly knew my classmates' faces, let alone their names.

"I… don't really know… the faces or names of my classmates… sorry." I felt bad. This girl recognized me, and even knew my name, but I didn't know who she was at all. *What if she gets upset? Am I being rude?*

As if sensing my worry, the girl smiled kindly in response. "Is that so? Well then, I guess I'll introduce myself again! I'm a first-year, in class three. My name is ———."

The girl introduced herself, and then stuck out her hand. I took it and she beamed widely as we shook hands.

"I hope we can be friends!"

The girl's hand, firmly gripping mine, was warm.

From that day on, my lonely life took a sharp, unexpected turn.

It was as she said — we became friendly with each other from that point on. The very next day, this strange tree-climbing girl approached me. Before I even realized it, she had become my very first friend.

And then...

"Acchan! Help me!" she said in a pathetic voice as she hugged me from behind.

"...What is it now?" I responded as calmly as I could.

"So there was that English assignment today... and I was supposed to do it, but I forgot all about it... I forgot the last one too! And the teacher told me that if I forgot again, he'd have me sweeping the halls!"

I stared at the face of my friend, who seemed close to tears, and sighed in exasperation. "You forget very... often." Even so, I reached into my bag and pulled out my English notebook. As soon as I handed it to her, a familiar smile returned to her face. "Make sure you return it before English class..."

"Ohhh! Acchan-sama! Thank you so very very much!" And with that she was off, dashing back to her table and writing in her notebook as fast as she could.

"Seems like you've gotten used to taking care of that wild monkey, Sasaki-san," said a classmate who'd seen this interaction.

"...Wild monkey?"

"Yes, wild monkey. It's been her nickname since she was in grade school. We were in the same class back then," the girl said, her smile bearing a hint of exasperation. "She'd always climb the trees in the schoolyard at break time. She does it a lot, even up in the hills. In fact, her rampant climbing caused rumors of a gigantic monkey living in those hills, way back then..."

"That's... something else."

Well, that made sense — if my newfound friend behaved like that in grade school, climbing trees in a skirt in middle school must have been pretty normal for her.

21

"And she'd forget her homework and notebooks, like, *all* the time. The teachers would get super mad at her, but she'd forget about it by the next day. And then she'd leave her homework behind *again*!"

"That's… really impressive…"

As my classmate said, my friend would be upset right after getting scolded by a teacher for forgetting something, but she'd always recover by the very next day. No matter how angry anyone got at her, she could somehow forget it after a good night's sleep. *I'm almost envious of how carefree she is…*

But even if my friend herself didn't mind, her habits caused a lot of trouble for others. "I guess the people around her have their hands full…" I said.

My classmate, however, suddenly looked more serious. "That's true. But you know… being around her is fun, isn't it?" she said, before grinning and starting to laugh. Before long, I was laughing too.

After that, I enjoyed hearing stories of my friend's zany antics.

And so, before I knew it, I started to make other friends — both friends of the wild monkey herself, and even other classmates. The wild monkey, who had been swinging around in the hills all this time, was eventually influenced by hobbies. She became interested in manga and anime too.

Perhaps it was because of this that she stopped visiting the hills so often. Her parents thanked me for this, though the conversation was a little awkward. "Thank you for turning that monkey back into a human," they said inexplicably.

Now, with a newfound friend who shared my interests, I found myself even more immersed in my hobby. Eventually, both of us became full-blown otaku, and the notorious wild monkey had become my closest friend.

Time passed, and our otaku friendship bloomed. Before long it was the third year of middle school, and we had started talking about attending a nearby high school together.

"Acchan... I c-can't... can't go on. I leave the rest... to you..." With that, my best friend slammed her textbook shut, before I smacked her on the head with a rolled pile of notes.

"Wh-What are you even saying...? It hasn't even been ten minutes since we started! If you keep this up, you'll fail the entrance exam and you'll have to wait one more year to start high school!"

"...Nghh... b-but... reading these endless lines in this thick reference book only makes me sleepy... I'm sure of it, the book must be cursed..."

She sighed deeply, trying to end our high school entrance exam study session after just ten minutes. Although she did well in sports, she was apparently hopeless in her studies. It wasn't like she was bad at studying — she just had no interest in it, and she was the kind of person who wouldn't even try to do things that bored her.

While I usually highlighted sections for her to study for school tests and the like, high school entrance exams weren't quite that simple. *What should I do...? At this rate, there's no way we'll end up in the same high school. She may even be held back a grade and have to study at a private tutoring center for a year. Is there some way for me to encourage this silly girl...?*

"Alright! When this test ends, I'll let you play all the otome games I've collected! All of them!"

"O... Otome games? You mean the..."

"Otome games" were my new favorite form of entertainment. I'd been buying a lot of them with the New Year's money I'd saved up. I'd been planning to share these games with her so we could discuss them in our free time.

However... seeing how unreliable their daughter was, her parents had decided that she couldn't be trusted with money. She only got the bare minimum for allowance, and even her New Year's money was transferred into a savings account. Since she couldn't buy anything expensive on her own, she didn't have any otome games or consoles to play them on. And I couldn't afford to buy two consoles, so I couldn't give one to her as a gift. I could only feel sad for her as she watched on enviously.

"...But... Acchan. You know I don't have any game consoles..." she said, visibly deflated.

But I smiled as encouragingly as I could at my friend. "I... I'll lend you mine! If you pass this test, I'll let you borrow them for a while! Then you can play!"

"...Oh... Acchan-sama...!" she said as she abruptly stood up, her sparkling eyes staring straight into mine. "Thank you, Acchan! I'll do whatever it takes to pass this high school entrance exam! For the otome games!" she declared passionately.

And so, she and I both passed our exams — although her motivations were somewhat questionable. We both worked hard, and ended up in the same high school.

There was yet another piece of good news waiting at the end of all this: To reward her unprecedented efforts at her studies, my friend's parents bought her a console in celebration, and for a while we were both happily lost in the world of otome games.

Once we went to high school, my number of otaku friends drastically increased. To buy our favorite games, my wild monkey friend and I started working part-time jobs. Some things didn't change, though — I would still cover for her when she forgot her assignments. Just like that, those peaceful days uneventfully passed us by.

The loneliness that I felt during grade school, and my isolation and inability to speak to people suddenly all seemed like a bad dream. Although she really was a troublemaker, I just couldn't feel resentful towards her, regardless of her antics. I was happy just spending my days by her side.

Back then, I believed that these days would go on forever, just like they always had.

By sheer coincidence, I left my phone at home that day. During our second year at high school, my friend and I had ended up in different classes — that was why I didn't realize what had happened.

Come to think of it... she didn't come find me to hang out today, huh... That was all I thought of it at the time.

And then, after school, I found out that I would never see her again.

Those peaceful days that I thought would go on forever suddenly ended — right there and then.

The funeral... the wake. I was there, but I didn't shed a single tear.

I couldn't believe that I would never see my friend again for as long as I lived. That I would never see her face again...

This is the wild monkey we were talking about! She'll come back somehow, she'll get out of it somehow, like she always has... right? Maybe she'll just...

After the funeral passed, the days went on as if nothing had ever happened. However, no matter how long I waited, my best friend never showed up again.

A few days later, I realized that I had an unread message on my phone. I had forgotten all about it until then. I was informed of the wake through mutual friends, and so I had hardly looked at my phone all this time.

When was it sent? I opened the message — and right there, on the screen, was the name of my best friend. I looked at the timestamp. It was the day of the accident, in the early hours of the morning.

"Acchan! I can't clear the route of the black-hearted sadist prince!!" The message was accompanied by a troubled face emoji. She must have been referring to a scenario in one of the otome games we played.

Her last message was... this. Up until her final moments... she really was... just like she'd always been.

I laughed in spite of myself. It was funny... and so I laughed. I laughed, and laughed, and laughed... until tears started flowing down my cheeks.

Before I knew it, more and more tears came. They wouldn't stop. It was like my eyes were melting from the sorrow — the tears just kept flowing.

Although she was gone from this world, I was no longer alone... because she had opened the door to a new world for me.

I held my smartphone tight to my chest. On its screen was the last message she had sent me. *That girl... that silly girl. She'll never come back, ever again.*

The days that I would live from now on... would be days without her. *I'll live. I'll live on... in this new world that she gifted me with.*

So… if life is like… the stories I read… If one day, my life were to end, and if I were to be reincarnated…

Then… please. I'd like to be with that girl… to be her friend. Just one more time.

And live those peaceful days, together with her… Just one more time.

"…Lady Sophia? Lady Sophia…"

Someone was calling out to me. Slowly, I opened my eyes — it was one of my family's maidservants, staring into my face with an expression of worry. She was the origin of the voice calling out to me.

"…Yes? What is it?" I asked, still feeling a bit dazed.

"…Well, you seemed to be calling out in your sleep… are you quite alright, young miss?"

"…Calling out? In my… sleep?" It was only after my confused response to the maidservant that I noticed that my cheeks were wet.

Ah… was I crying? It somehow feels like… I know the reason why. "…I had… a very sad dream. I suppose that was why I… was speaking in my sleep."

"A dream, Lady Sophia?"

"Yes… it was a really, really sad dream… But I seem to have forgotten all about it… upon waking up."

Yes. Although I couldn't remember the details, the sadness in my heart was unmistakable. It was a most… sorrowful dream.

"I was probably… remembering. Remembering the past…"

"...I see. The past..." The maidservant's expression seemed to freeze up in response to my mumbling. Her response was conspicuously vague.

Up until only a few years ago, I was seen as strange... perhaps even abnormal. I was gossiped about and discriminated against, and in response, shut myself up in my room. The maidservant probably assumed I was thinking of that.

"...Um. It was not about me being a shut-in... The dream, I mean. It was... further in the past. A dream from a long, long time ago..."

The maidservant's expression changed into one of puzzlement. But I supposed that would be natural... I was still merely a child. How could I have memories from a time long gone...?

Honestly, I didn't have an explanation... All I knew was how sad it was. A sad, sorrowful dream I couldn't remember...

But yet, it felt like I knew, somehow, that it happened a long time ago. Yes, a long, long time ago... Although I couldn't remember the details of my dream, I felt a profound sense of sorrow and pain gnawing away at my heart.

"Lady Sophia, you're due to visit Claes Manor today!" said my maidservant, trying to cheer me up.

Hearing those words made me feel relieved — if only just a little.

That's right. I'm going to visit Katarina today. I selected some great books to recommend to her. I wonder if she'll like them? I could feel the rest of my sorrow slowly fading away as I continued thinking of Katarina.

I dressed up, had my breakfast, and prepared to leave the house. I then headed over to Claes Manor, with my brother Nicol in tow, as usual.

Upon reaching Claes Manor, I saw Katarina in the gardens — where she usually was. She was with her adopted brother, Keith.

"Keith! This is definitely an edible mushroom, I can tell!"

"No, Big Sister. We don't have detailed knowledge of the mushrooms that sprout from these trees. These mystery mushrooms are definitely not edible…"

"No, no! What are you talking about? They're definitely edible. After all, they smell just like shiitake mushrooms do! This is definitely some variant of shiitake. I just know it!"

"Wh-What is this 'shiitake,' Big Sister? In any case, please put that mystery mushroom down. You must absolutely not eat it! It could cause a terrible stomach ache!"

"Ah, no no. You see Keith, you don't know that until you've actually eaten it! Ah… Sophia!"

It would seem that Katarina and Keith were engaged in an enthusiastic conversation. There was a large smile on Katarina's face as she turned to face me.

I could feel the last vestiges of sadness peel away from my aching heart. It was really fortunate that I had attended that royal tea party, all those years ago… and that I met with Katarina Claes on that very day.

"Lady Katarina… I-I've brought some new recommendations with me… they are most interesting books…"

"Really?! Thank you so much, Sophia!" Katarina was jumping for joy as I held out the books I had been carrying.

The days I spend with Katarina are full of joy. I feel really fortunate to have made friends with her.

Before I knew it, there were no longer any traces of the sadness that I had felt just moments ago. It was all gone… just like that.

As spring came to pass, it was finally time for me to attend classes at the Academy of Magic — the school where teens with magical powers would study to improve their skills.

Once magic-users turned fifteen years old, we were required to attend classes at the academy. For two years, students from all walks of life would study there while living in the academy's dormitories.

The academy was funded and run by the kingdom, and the dormitories were considered top-class. It was a very large campus — with the school building itself, dormitories for both students and teachers, magical research facilities, and things like that.

There was a good reason the Powers That Be funded this big of an academy. Those with magical abilities and their magic spells were huge assets to the kingdom. After all, there were few people with magical aptitude in the surrounding lands. There were some here and there, but they were pretty rare. Our kingdom, on the other hand, was abnormal when it came to how many of our people had the innate potential for magic. These magical powers were used for the kingdom's expansion and progress.

This academy was the result of the fortunes gathered by the kingdom's magically capable population, so that the next generation would be guided on the use of their talents and would then benefit the kingdom in return. This was what led to the founding of the Academy of Magic.

At this school, those with great magical power commanded respect. In fact, their influence was said to be second only to the king himself. These people were promised seats in the Magical Ministry — a powerful organization of mages.

And so, fifteen-year-old boys and girls from all over the kingdom would enroll at the academy this year. Most of them were nobles; in fact, most of them came from families standing on the top of aristocratic society. This might have been the reason behind a unique social norm in the kingdom: that the presence of magical powers would determine a person's social standing. Some children with great magical strength would be adopted by nobles on higher rungs of society. And a lot of nobles achieved elevated status once their exceptional magical talent was discovered at the academy.

But of course, not all who were born with magical aptitude were nobles. While it was rare, this power would occasionally appear in a commoner. In those cases, even if the prospective student were of common birth, they would be allowed to enroll at the academy as long as they could use magic.

From what I'd heard, the last time a commoner student stepped through the academy's gates was around a decade ago. But I knew this streak would end with my incoming class, since a commoner would be attending the academy.

Maria Campbell. Although she was born a commoner, she could use the extraordinary Light Magic. Amongst the five magical elements, Light was the strongest and most rare. In fact, there were only a handful of users in the kingdom, from what I'd been told.

Although she wasn't a noble, Maria was one of the few who were capable of "wielding the Light." Of course, everyone's attention was trained on her during the academy's entrance ceremony. I ended up following their gazes and looking straight at her too.

31

She was a beautiful young lady with her flowing, blonde hair and crystal-clear azure eyes. In fact, it was easy to fall for her beauty if you stared at her for just a little bit too long. A commoner, and yet a Wielder of Light. Maria Campbell was, without doubt, the most exceptional girl in this academy — no, perhaps the entire kingdom.

Before my eyes was none other than the protagonist of *Fortune Lover*. With the protagonist's debut, the game would now finally begin. It would take one year from this point in time for the game to end. Hence begins the Grand Strategy of Katarina Claes — The War Against Catastrophic Bad Ends.

"Catastrophic Bad Ends will never get the better of me…!" I said, breathing in deeply as I clenched my fists, preparing myself for the storm that was to come.

The academy had multiple dorm buildings and wings, each one meant for a certain rank of nobility. There were separate sections for students who came from the ranks of royalty, dukes, marquesses, counts, viscounts, barons, and so on. Students from royal and duke families were rare, and some school years had no such students at all. But this year, there were plenty. I heard that students from lesser noble families were forced to take rooms in buildings that were one step lower than usual due to the lack of space.

Luckily, my friends and I were pretty high on the nobility scale, and we had all ended up in the same dormitory building. There were gender-segregated areas in the dormitories — one wing for the boys, another for the girls. But there were shared areas too, such as the dining hall or the student lounge, where students could mingle with their peers. And we were allowed to visit a classmate of the opposite gender in their quarters as long as we had permission.

Lastly, we were allowed to roam freely on the grounds of the academy as long as we returned to the dormitories by nightfall. And this rule was hardly enforced unless we were discovered wandering around in the middle of the night.

The reason for this was simple — the academy grounds were completely safe. It was a walled community, closely guarded and patrolled by security forces. And so I didn't feel trapped by my new life; in fact, I felt like I had a new sense of freedom. I could see my friends any time I wanted, just like I did back at the manor.

A few days had passed since the inauguration ceremony, and today, Jeord had invited me to his room after dinner. "Katarina, I have procured some rare and exquisite candies. Do visit me in my room after our meal," he said.

However, Keith had somehow gotten wind of this, and he showed up when I was preparing to leave to insist that he come along as well. He sounded a little desperate. *I guess Keith can't resist rare candies either. I should make sure to invite him next time.*

So Keith and I made our way over to Jeord's quarters, and as promised, rows of delicious-looking goodies were arranged on a table. The sheer variety was astounding — there were so many kinds of candies! *I wonder where I should start...*

As I mooned over the food, I spotted Jeord and Keith talking together from the corner of my eye.

"I had only extended an invitation to Katarina, if I do recall. Why are you here with her, Keith Claes?"

"Ah, Prince Jeord. I had requested Big Sister's servants to inform me should any... developments, come to pass. You see, my sister does not quite have a good sense of danger, no matter how much I warn her. To think that something would happen so early into the school term... It was wise to have depended upon her maidservants."

Oh! What rare candies! I've never even seen some of these before. They look so delicious! I want to bite into them now! But Jeord and Keith were up to one of their usual happy little talks, and still hadn't taken their seats. *Ugh! Quickly! When can I sink my teeth into them?!*

"Would that not be overstepping your boundaries, Keith Claes? After all, you are but an adopted brother..."

"Prince Jeord! Prince Jeord! Can I... Can I eat this? Now?" Unable to hold myself back any longer, I interrupted their conversation.

"Ah, but of course. I prepared it all for you, after all. Eat as much as you like, Katarina," Jeord said with a somewhat twitchy smile on his face. I gratefully accepted his offer, and promptly planted myself in the closest chair.

Keith seemed to have a similarly twitchy smile. *They're probably thinking about how I only think about food. But... how can they blame me?! Look at these scrumptious treats laid out before me! No one in their right mind could resist!*

And so the three of us, finally, started having our snacks and after-dinner tea.

"Come to think of it, I just met that girl — the one with the Light Magic, prior to this little tea-party of ours," Jeord said, suddenly changing the subject.

At that very moment, my cheeks had been stuffed full of food, and I was washing it down with a hearty gulp of tea... But when Jeord spoke, all the tea I had just drank immediately tried to come spurting back out. Fortunately, I was quick enough to seal my lips shut, and so averted a disaster. I was two seconds away from coloring Prince Jeord and his tablecloth a nice shade of tea-brown.

That was close... Relieved, I sank into my seat.

However Keith, who was seated next to me, seemed to be interested in Jeord's statement. "Ah, yes. Would she be the commoner who's the center of attention right now?"

"Yes indeed. I encountered her by chance during a stroll through the grounds earlier today..."

A stroll? A stroll of the grounds and... Ah! An event! Jeord has encountered the protagonist!

In the original setting of *Fortune Lover*, the protagonist character, curious about her new surroundings, attempts to take a walk around the academy grounds. However, the academy is bigger than she'd thought, and she gets lost. To get herself out of her newfound predicament, the protagonist then climbs a tree while dressed in a skirt, thinking that the view would help her figure out where she was.

It is then that Jeord, the fairytale, blonde-haired and blue-eyed prince, appears. The protagonist then blushes, having been seen by the prince in such an embarrassing state. The prince would then become interested in this silly, tree-climbing tomboy of a protagonist, and end up escorting her back to her dormitory.

...And here he was, telling me of the sequence of events, just like it had been in the game. I could only listen in despair. *This was exactly how it turned out in the* Fortune Lover *scenario...* After this meeting, Jeord would start getting interested in the protagonist, and very soon, he would fall for her.

"Oh? So there are other women who would climb trees, other than Big Sister?"

"Yes... it was a first for me, as well. I have long since gotten used to Katarina's antics, and hardly see it as anything strange... But the girl herself seemed embarrassed at having been witnessed in such a state."

"…I agree, Prince Jeord. Under normal circumstances, any lady would be shocked if she were to be seen climbing a tree in a skirt… Most ladies would not simply say, 'Oh, don't worry about it! I'm a professional when it comes to tree-climbing!' And especially not in that confident tone…"

"Well, I do say that Katarina is the exception, as opposed to the norm. Ah, but that is yet another one of Katarina's charms… Hmm? Are you listening, Katarina?"

Ugh… Katarina Claes, Jeord's fiancée of convenience to stave off other suitors… Once Jeord falls in love with the protagonist, she'll be in the way!

"Are you listening to me, Katarina? Ah… I suppose we have lost her, Keith. She does not appear to be taking in anything we are saying. She really does have a knack for spacing out, does she not?"

"…That is unfortunately the case, Prince Jeord."

Ah… this is bad, this is really bad! It's only been a few days since the start of school, and Jeord is already being charmed by the protagonist's wiles! She's too powerful! I can feel the Catastrophic Bad Ends creeping up behind me!

The more I thought about it, the more disturbed I became, sinking into my own world. Amidst all the panic, I forgot to check one very important thing — the progression of Jeord and the protagonist's relationship…!

"Ah, now is a good time, Big Sister. We should return to our quarters," Keith said as I continued to mumble, lost in my thoughts. It seemed like the two of them found my confusion amusing. "Big Sister… We are no longer back home at the manor. You really should not be picking up strange things and assuming that they are edible…"

"It is as he says, Katarina. You are already fifteen years of age. You should really stop picking up strange things off the ground, let alone consuming them on a regular basis."

It appeared that both Keith and Jeord had decided that my behavior was because I'd eaten another unidentified mushroom or something. To be fair, that had happened more than a few times before...

I did have one issue with their assumption, though. *I don't "pick up strange things off the ground!" I only "pick" fruits off of trees and plants! That's not the same thing!*

...Also, in the dozen or so times that I've done that, I only got crippling stomach aches like twice. So there.

Unable to clear up the misunderstanding, I sulked all the way back to my room.

"Actually, Big Sister, I too have met with that very same girl that Prince Jeord was talking about."

Only a few days after the shocking revelation from Jeord, my brother Keith had the same kind of experience.

Keith, who had come to meet me so we could go to classes together after breakfast, told me this casually. Thankfully, this time I didn't have any tea in my mouth to launch across the room. But even so...

"...WhaaaAA?!"

I could only choke out a weird half-shout.

"B-Big Sister... what's wrong?" Keith said, approaching me with a shaken expression in response to my strange vocalization.

"Y-You… h-haven't been picking up girls, have you?!"

In *Fortune Lover*, Keith and the protagonist's meeting was triggered by a pick-up line from Keith himself. Because he was a dangerous playboy in the original setting, he always had a smooth line for any woman he came across. In the original scenario, he meets the rumored Light-wielding girl by chance, and out of sheer curiosity, tries to charm her too.

"…Hmm? What is this… 'picking up' of girls, Big Sister…?"

"…Ah? You don't know what picking up means? Um… How do I put it… seducing women into doing depraved things…"

"D-Depraved?! Wha… Why would I do anything like that!" Keith shouted, his face flushed red.

Hmm. I suppose Keith as he is now would never think of doing anything like that. While he was a despicable playboy in the original script of the game, Keith had long since become a completely different person thanks to my guidance. He was now a gracious gentleman… though he still unknowingly stole the heart of every woman he met.

I had to find out more. Approaching Keith, who was still shaking his head rapidly with his face flushed, I presented him with another question: "Alright, then what happened?"

"She was walking ahead of me, Big Sister, and then she dropped her h-handkerchief… and I picked it up for her… that's all…"

"…Handkerchief…" *That's right!*

In *Fortune Lover*, Keith fails in his first attempt to seduce the protagonist, who turns him down. That only makes him more interested in her — a woman who would refuse his advances. After that she would turn to leave, only to accidentally drop her handkerchief as she walks away. Keith would then approach the protagonist again a few days later, once again attempting to charm her with his wiles. From what I could remember, he says... *"Here, this is yours, right? If you want it back, come have some fun with me..."*

"...So. What happened to that handkerchief...?" Fearfully, I posed my next question.

"...What do you mean, Big Sister? I just gave it back to her after she had dropped it..."

"I... see..." It would seem that Keith hadn't held onto that handkerchief... which meant that he had no intention of approaching her with it later. But I had learned my lesson ever since my failure during the Jeord Tea-Time Incident. I had to be sure of this.

"...Well. So you met that Light-wielding girl, right...? How did you feel about her, Keith...?"

"How did I feel...? She was just a pleasant girl. She thanked me formally for returning her handkerchief to her..." Keith responded, seemingly confused by my persistent questions.

Argh! That isn't it, Keith! That's not what I am asking about at all!

...You leave me no choice, little brother! A direct approach is needed!

"Urgh! That's not what I wanted to know! Keith. How did you feel about meeting Maria? Did you fall hopelessly in love with her at first sight?! At the sight of Maria's incredible beauty?!" I demanded, placing my hands on Keith's shoulders, holding him in place with a death grip, even though he was a lot taller than me.

Keith's eyes widened. "...?! F-Fall in l-love?? Whatever do you mean...?"

Ah, that's the first time I've seen that in a while. I hadn't seen Keith this surprised since he was first adopted into the Claes household. *I'm right on the mark... there's no mistaking it! Keith already has budding feelings for Maria Campbell, Wielder of Light!*

"I see. I see... So you already have feelings for Miss Campbell, yes?"

"Eh...? Big Sister...? I... I don't... What are you talking about...?"

I tightened my grip on Keith's shoulders. "No. No... it's fine. You don't have to hide it, Keith. Aren't we brother and sister?! So... I'd just like to say one thing, Keith... That your Big Sister would never try to come between you and your love!"

In the original events of *Fortune Lover*, Katarina cannot accept the fact that Keith, who was adopted by a duke, would dare develop a relationship with the commoner Maria. As a result, she repeatedly gets in the way of their relationship. In the end, her behavior would cause Keith to erase her. But of course, as I was now, I had no intention of getting between them at all!

"I support you, Keith! I approve of the budding love between you and Miss Campbell! Big Sister will always be on your side! She will never get in the way of your romance!" I declared profusely, all the while staring straight into Keith's eyes.

For some reason, however, all traces of emotion faded from Keith's face. *Is it me, or does Keith look a lot worse off than he did earlier?* "...Keith?"

Then Anne's voice rang out from behind me, shaking me out of my tirade. "Young miss, please... if you say any more than that... I think Master Keith is at his limit..."

At his limit...? Ah! I see! It was only then that I realized I had been shaking Keith back and forth this entire time as I spoke, all the while trapping him in my death grip. As we had just had our breakfast a few minutes ago, he was probably feeling sick from being shaken so hard! *Even though I didn't mean to, I've done a terrible thing!*

"Oh! I am so sorry, Keith! I shouldn't have shaken you so hard right after your breakfast! Should I help you to the infirmary? You can't go to class while you're sick!" I said, apologizing for my blunder.

Keith, still looking very sickly, reassured me that he was fine.

"But... you don't look very good, Keith!"

"No, Big Sister... it is not that I am unwell... I am physically alright, but... it is more of a mental... mental problem..." For some reason, Keith started muttering about things I couldn't understand. But he firmly refused to go to the infirmary, assuring me that he wasn't sick.

So instead, we met up with our usual group of friends before heading off to the academy's school building. But Keith didn't seem to recover on our way there.

Ohh, I got carried away again and ended up shaking my brother too hard, and just after he had a full breakfast! I really am terrible.

Lessons in the Academy of Magic were organized like this: Half of our classes were lectures, and the other half were practical training. The lectures were on familiar topics that I'd been taught by my tutors like history, plus magical theory and general studies on spells. The practical side involved us training our magic by casting real spells. Lectures were typically held in the morning, and practicums in the afternoon. In between was our break time.

There were dedicated classrooms for first-year students, but there was no seating chart, so we could sit wherever we wanted. I was flanked by Mary and Sophia. Jeord, Keith, and Alan were seated in the row behind us. Although Keith had been sitting in his usual spot for the whole morning, he didn't seem to be able to concentrate at all.

He was probably still suffering from Shaken-Keith Syndrome... But of course, I usually fell asleep during lecture times, so I didn't really know if Keith usually focused during these lessons.

With our lectures of the day over, it was time for lunch break — and almost as if on cue, Keith now seemed to be back to his usual self.

"All this started with me underestimating the enemy... her relative thickness and penchant for misunderstandings... all I have to do is simply... must press on... the attack from now on..." he murmured, holding my hands tight as his beautiful face came almost uncomfortably close to mine.

What's this all about? Anyway, he seemed a lot better now, so that was good.

But even so... Keith, who's already so popular with girls, is going around holding their hands and staring into their faces like this? He's truly fearsome... If he goes on like this, even the purest of girls will fly into a frenzy!

Except me, of course, since I'm his sister.

I know I'm the one who made him sick in the first place, but still, Keith can't go around doing these things so casually! As his big sister, I have to be on the lookout for him!

Anyway, the charm of the protagonist, Maria, was definitely strong. She had caught Jeord's interest and bewitched Keith all in a matter of days. She really was impressive.

Since it had come to this, I felt that it was time for a fresh revision of my strategies... And so it came to be that we had yet another strategy meeting in our dormitory room that night.

We now officially commence another Catastrophic Bad End Avoidance Strategy Meeting. On the agenda this time should be "The impressive charm of the protagonist, Miss Maria Campbell," if I may humbly suggest.

Meeting chairwoman: Katarina Claes.

Meeting representative: Katarina Claes.

Meeting secretary: Katarina Claes.

"Well then everyone, please let me hear your thoughts."

"If I may."

"Yes, of course. Go on, Miss Katarina Claes."

"As it was stated in the agenda… the protagonist, Miss Maria Campbell's charm is way too strong! It defies our wildest imagination! It seems that she has already piqued Jeord's interest, and charmed poor Keith!"

"That would appear to be the case, yes. As expected of the protagonist…"

"However… would it not be fair to say that Jeord has yet to fall for her?"

"No, think about it! Jeord, who hardly shows interest in anything, was interested in this girl's behavior! It is only a matter of time before he's charmed too!"

"Is that really the case? Perhaps the Jeord in the original *Fortune Lover* setting would feel that way. But Jeord as he is now often gives me advice about my fields and crops, and brings me various types of candies and snacks… Although he still does get bored with certain things."

"Hmm… I suppose you could be right. However, isn't it a first for Jeord to be specifically interested in a certain person? Jeord is always all about Katarina! Have you ever heard him say anything about anyone else in our presence?"

"That's right! Maria is the first girl that Jeord has so openly displayed an interest in... Perhaps it's only a matter of time before he falls for her too..."

"I knew it... Maria's wiles are truly... wiley."

"At this rate, even Alan and Nicol will soon fall prey to her charms."

"I'm afraid so..."

"Hmm. Is that really how it looks to you?"

"Huh?! What do you mean?"

"While it's true that Maria is academically and magically skilled in the setting of *Fortune Lover*, and is also incredibly beautiful... if those are the only factors, Mary and Sophia will both give her a run for her money!"

"Wha?!"

"Both Alan and Nicol's rival characters are skilled in academics and magic, and they are extremely beautiful! Even Maria couldn't easily gain an advantage over them!"

"Oh, I see! Given Mary and Sophia's strengths, they won't lose that easily!"

"Yes, those two will certainly put up a fight! If anyone were to fail in their love endeavors, it would be Katarina Claes, who is bad at both her studies and magic!"

"Exactly. The only one who would lose out when it came to love is Katarina... and that would be a good thing."

"A good thing indeed."

"...Hold on. Wait... THAT'S NO GOOD! If Katarina loses, that's no good at all! Won't she be headed straight for a Catastrophic Bad End?!"

"Oh no, that's true isn't it?! That wouldn't be good at all!"

"...It is as you say... we can't exactly lose either... But everyone, calm down for a moment. Would a girl lacking in both academic and magical skill, as well as having the face of a villainess... ever be able to beat a pretty noble lady who was both well-read and magically inclined?"

"..."

"..."

"...Let's plant crops and till some fields! We could set up a farm! Just like what was recommended in 'On Agricultural Considerations and Recommendations'! We were told that farming is all about accumulating experience! Even if we are exiled, our experience would contribute to our life as a humble farmer! As I thought, we cannot possibly stop our fieldwork just because we're attending the academy!"

"That's right! And if Jeord should ever come at us with his blade, claiming that we are in the way of his love... then all we have to do is practice throwing the snakes that he's so fearful of! We have to keep up with snake-tossing practice!"

"Also, we should get permission from our teachers to continue our swordplay training! Even if we spook Jeord with a projectile snake, it will all end if we can't dodge his blows!"

"Exactly! That too!"

"Well then... tomorrow, we'll ask if the academy would allow us to set up a small field on the grounds, practice tossing projectile snakes, and continue our training in the ways of the sword. Does that cover everything?"

"Yes."

With that, another Catastrophic Bad End Avoidance Strategy Meeting had come to an end. We did not, however, come to any new or astounding solutions…

"…I suppose I can ask the teachers if I can have permission to till a small field in the academy grounds first thing in the morning…" And with those thoughts in mind, I slowly drifted off to sleep, in a bed much smaller than the one I was used to back home.

A few days later, I found myself in an isolated corner of the academy grounds, hoe in hand. Raising it above my hand in a familiar pose, I tilled the earth with well-practiced motions.

"Young miss… is this really a flower field?" Anne asked, suspicion plain in her voice and on her face.

"Yes, of course! A field of pretty flowers! Aren't I planting these because both you and Keith said that crops are definitely not allowed in these fields?"

Although I'd been full of enthusiasm for a fresh field of crops in the academy, Keith and Anne were really against it. *"A noble lady working fields at the manor is one thing, but doing the same on academy grounds…? Absolutely not!"* they'd said, and I'd replied… *"Well, how about a field of flowers, then?"* That was what I wrote in my application to the academy.

Weirdly, flower gardening was apparently seen as an acceptable hobby for nobles, and I soon got approval from the school to go ahead with my little project. That was why I could be here now, working this field. But Anne didn't seem very convinced.

"But… young miss. I really do not feel that those seedlings you just planted over there are flowers of any kind…"

"Don't be silly, Anne. What do you mean? They're flowers! Look at them! Over here we have cucumber flowers, and over there we have eggplant flowers…"

"…Young miss. In other words, you are confirming what I have seen. These are seedlings for crops, are they not?"

"Hmm. Yes, I guess they'll end up as crops in the end, but before that, their flowers do bloom, like all flowers do!" I said, puffing out my chest with pride.

Anne could only stare at me, sighing deeply in response. "To think that you had agreed to it so quickly, young miss…"

"But I've already planted and transported the seedlings, see? Isn't it great?" I asked, glancing up at Anne. Once again, Anne sighed, even deeper this time.

"…I understand. However… you would do well to be careful. The other students and the academy cannot find out about the fact that this field is actually full of crops…"

"Thank you, Anne!" *Yes! I've done it, and gained Anne's approval!* Now all I had to do was convince Keith, and then there wouldn't be any more complaints about my field.

"…On another note, young miss… that hoe and those overalls of yours… I cannot help but feel like I have seen them before somewhere…"

"Oh, this? But of course you would. These are the same hoe and overalls that I was using back at the manor!"

A strange look crept into Anne's expression as she heard those words. "…It is as I thought… However, if memory serves, I had specifically left that hoe and those overalls back at Claes Manor…"

"You sure did! And after I'd gone through all the trouble of hiding them in with my things… and then you removed them! You left me no choice, so I sent word back to the manor to Grandpa Tom! It was he who sent me these items in the post!"

"...An unexpected betrayal, Mister Tom..." Anne soon fell silent after muttering something I couldn't quite hear.

Raising the hoe over my head once more, I continued my work. Compared to the fields back home, this one was much smaller and less tidy. I didn't have very much free time during the day since I had so many lectures, so I had to make the most of my time when I was here.

While there was plenty of complaining and sighing from Keith, I managed to convince him too. However, it didn't take long for my friends to find out about the existence of this small field.

Upon seeing me with my gardening overalls and hoe, Alan started laughing so hard that he doubled over, hugging his stomach. "Wow, you're still doing that? Here? Really?"

Jeord, who was standing next to him, seemed to have his gaze fixed onto the ground as his shoulders shook. Mary, Sophia, and Nicol were surprised at first, but quickly offered me their help if I needed it.

There was one year left in this otome game scenario. Today, too, I was working hard in the fields — all for the sake of overcoming the Catastrophic Bad Ends that awaited me.

As the weeks went by, I slowly got used to life at the Academy of Magic. The content of the lectures wasn't too difficult compared to what I'd learned from my personal tutors, but unfortunately, this meant that my habit of sleeping in class only got worse. Our practicums were taught by specialists in different fields of magic, and their lessons were always interesting. Sadly, my magical powers didn't improve; I was only able to use my usual "Dirt Bump" spell.

While the other students didn't speak to me much because of my high social standing, everyone was polite and pleasant. The only ones who had issues with me were noble ladies who didn't like the fact that I was engaged to Jeord. They would glare and whisper mean things about me when I passed by them.

There was one particular noble lady who disliked me even more than the others. I found out later that she was originally the one that everyone expected Jeord to marry before I came along. Whenever I saw her, this girl would always say something like "Someone like you is not worthy of Jeord." But I didn't really care about the grumbling and stares of a few girls.

My days at the academy went on normally until the time came for our evaluation tests, which were designed to gauge the academic and magical capabilities of each student. This was something I remembered from the game. All we had to do was repeat what our tutors had taught us for the academic portion, and cast our most powerful spell under the supervision of a teacher for the magical potion.

The tests came to an uneventful end, and just as expected, Keith, Jeord, Alan, Mary, and Sophia were all ranked at the top. The test rankings were monopolized by my group of friends. *Naturally! I wouldn't expect anything less from them.*

There was also one other person at the top of the rankings: Maria, the protagonist of *Fortune Lover*. Since she was a commoner, there was no way she grew up with private tutors like we did. In fact, she was studying at a public school near her home before she came here. And yet, she performed much better than the majority of noble students. No surprises there.

My own rankings were... pretty much average. I was right in the middle. *Hooray for being average!* I cheered internally, congratulating myself on my achievement. *Come to think of it, the results were exactly like in* Fortune Lover. *First was Jeord, and coming in second was Maria. Alan, who was in third place, originally hated the fact that Maria had beaten him. But now...*

"Ain't a competition, is it? Some people are good at some things, and some people aren't. Compatibility, right? I don't get caught up in things like that," he said casually.

Alan wasn't showing any sign of hostility towards Maria. In fact, he didn't dwell on the subject at all, and instead brought up something new.

"Yesterday, a teacher approached me at violin practice and asked if I would consider performing on the academy grounds. So... what do you think?"

"I think that's a great idea. Lots of people have been missing your performances since you went to the academy."

"...What about you? Do you want to listen too?"

"Oh, sure. Of course I do."

"I see. Well then. Guess I'll hold a performance or two on the grounds..." And with that, Alan turned and left with a happy expression on his face. This was a far cry from how he would storm off in the game, upset at the test results.

I was noticing moments like this more and more. While some parts of the game's original script remained, there were plenty of changes. Another example of a major difference was the selection of the academy's student council. This group, which had been part of the academy since its establishment, was apparently "an organization which brings about positive change and enrichment to the academy via effective self-governance by students."

Actually, the activities of the council were what you might expect, like helping teachers in class and settling disputes amongst students. It seemed like it mainly existed to do a variety of odd jobs.

But the selection of the council members was very different from how it was done in my school from my previous life. There were no votes or campaigning or anything like that. Instead, the top students from the evaluation test were conscripted to become part of the council, and that was that.

Forcing students to participate in the council seemed kind of unfair to me, but most students didn't see it this way. It was apparently an honor to be selected, since it meant you were the best in the school. So almost everyone at the top of the list happily accepted their assignment. These chosen few were admired and envied by the student population.

Keith and my friends, having scored very well in the evaluation test, were all selected for the council — along with Maria, the protagonist. So far, this all lined up with the game's script. But the big difference was that I, at the insistence of my friends, was also included in the council. When they all asked this in unison, the teacher in charge seemed flustered. I guess they were concerned that I'd feel left out if they were all on the council and I wasn't.

Anne seemed to feel the same way. She didn't accompany me when I went out to go to classes and such, since her job was only to take care of me in the dorms. Still, when I went off to work in the fields after classes, I was followed by her mutters of "Whatever would the young miss do if she were left up to her own devices…?"

While I was happy that my friends cared about me so much, I didn't mind being on my own. I loved spending time with them, of course, but I was fine with having some alone time. I tried to explain this to everyone, but before I knew it, I had somehow gained the rights to enter the student council chambers, which would have otherwise been off-limits to me. In fact, they urged me strongly to visit them there. Almost like I didn't have a choice...

Apparently, my friends had done something about the rules of the council chambers. But none of them would tell me exactly what happened, even when I asked, so I guess I'll never know.

And so, for one reason or another, I soon found myself visiting the student council chambers on a regular basis.

"This way please, Lady Katarina," the student before me said, smiling as he offered me a cup of tea.

"Th-Thank you very much."

This person was a second-year student, the top of his class, and the student council president. He had a shock of red hair and ash-grey eyes, and had a warm, friendly personality that reminded me of a puppy. This charming boy was just as eye-catching as the others in the council.

The vice-president was Nicol Ascart, the Alluring Count. On paper, the council members were selected for their academic and magical capabilities, but when I looked around the room... I couldn't help but think that their looks were taken into account too.

Nicol and the president were the only two second-year students left on the council — the rest of the seven positions were taken by the newly appointed first-years. According to the president, they originally had seven of their classmates on the council. But apparently some kind of trouble went down, with Nicol at the center of it all, and the other members ended up resigning their posts.

The president himself seemed to have some resistance to Nicol's magnetism, probably because he was so handsome himself. But still... the Alluring Count's charms were truly fearsome.

Because of that incident, the new first-years joining the diminished council was great news for the president, especially since they all came equipped with Nicol-resistance.

And so I was welcomed into the student council chambers on my visits, even though I had nothing to do with anything going on there other than the fact that I was friends with its new members. No one here seemed to be bothered with my sudden appearance, though. They even served me freshly brewed tea.

Due to their warm welcome, I started coming more often. Before long, it was like I was a member of the council myself. Well, maybe it would be more accurate to say that my caring friends had ensured that I became a member.

As a result of my entry into the council's social circle, I gained opportunities to interact with other members too, namely...

"Please feel free to try some of these too, Lady Claes, if they are to your liking."

My heart couldn't help but skip a beat at the sight of the beautiful girl before me, offering up a tray of sweets as I sipped on the tea that the president had brewed for me.

"Th-Thank you, Miss Campbell."

Maria Campbell smiled slightly at my stuttered expression of gratitude. Yes, I was speaking to the protagonist herself. On my many visits to the council chambers, I ended up spending a lot of time with Maria. We had become friendly with each other, and now she would always welcome me with a smile and a tray of sweets in her hands.

I had only thought of her as the game's protagonist up until that point, but as I got to know her more, I started to see her for who she really was — a kind and gentle soul. She was talented and empathetic, already an all-around amazing young lady. But even though she was so impressive, she was never arrogant. Instead, she was humble and gracious. She really was a wonderful, charming girl.

Why did the original Katarina Claes hate this gentle girl so much? I couldn't wrap my head around it. *I mean, it was probably because of Maria's charm ensnaring all her crushes and friends.*

As those thoughts passed through my mind, I idly popped a pastry into my mouth. *Guh?! W-Wow! So impressive! What a delicious morsel.*

"These pastries are... quite delicious." I said, turning to Maria.

"Yes, they are! These sweets were given to the council from the students of the academy."

Ah, so that's where they're from. Since the council was admired by the student body, a number of gifts would arrive for its members on a regular basis. And since there were many admirers who hailed from high-ranking noble families, the gifts were naturally expensive and high-quality.

Ah, speaking of food... "Would you be interested in baking some sweets and bringing them here to share with us, Miss Campbell?"

In the original setting of *Fortune Lover*, Maria's hobby was baking. In fact, her homemade sweets were often shared with the other members of the council. Although they tasted quite different from the high-class treats that were often sent to the council chamber, the homemade charm of her pastries would seize the stomach and heart of any potential love interest.

The game's illustrations of Maria's homemade sweets were impossibly lifelike. I could almost taste them. I remembered feeling so inspired that I ended up in a convenience store, trying to find food that looked just like the game.

Now that I was on the other side of the screen, I could still picture Maria's freshly baked sweets... But now I could eat them all in person! Or at least, that's what I thought as I eagerly awaited her answer.

"...Huh?" Instead, Maria Campbell stood, frozen on the spot.

Does she think I'm threatening her?! Like, "Bake me food and present them to me, or else!" Panicking, I acted quickly to resolve the misunderstanding. "Ah, no, um. You see, you don't have to make them if you don't want to, I wasn't..."

"...Um. Lady Claes... how is it that you know about my baking...?"

Ah, is that what she's confused about? But she had a point. She hadn't revealed to any of us that she liked baking. Even the player of the game would only discover this after Maria borrows a small corner of the school kitchen to bake by herself.

The subject of baking came up in all of the potential routes of the game. It would appear once the protagonist was close enough with a love interest, who would then say something like "Well then, maybe you could make some for me too."

Judging by Maria's reaction, however, it seemed like she hadn't told anyone about her hobby yet. *Hmm. What should I say? I can't just be like, "Oh, I saw you baking cookies in this one game I played."*

"Umm... Uh. Th-That was... because I heard about it from the chefs of the dining hall, so..."

"...I see."

Not exactly the smoothest excuse, but Maria seemed convinced. I could relax... for now.

"…It is as you say, Lady Claes… Although I did borrow a small space in the kitchens for personal use, I just made a small amount… Also, the baked goods I make are hardly worthy of the palates of those on the council, so…" Maria said, looking at the professionally made sweets still seated on their tray. She seemed troubled.

That made sense. With the high-class food made from famous patisseries lined up on the table before us, it must be daunting for an amateur baker to display their own work alongside them. Not to mention that cooking and baking were strange hobbies for noble ladies to begin with. They usually had chefs and other kitchen staff to prepare meals.

Of course I, as the daughter of Duke Claes, couldn't cook or bake at all. I was a noble lady of well-established traditions and upbringing, after all. The kitchens were off-limits to me at Claes Manor. When my memories had first come back to me, I'd sneaked into the kitchen several times to snack and try the different ingredients and spices. I even tried to cook some of the mystery mushrooms I found in the gardens… But eventually, the head chef decided he'd had enough.

"The kitchens are a dangerous place, young miss, with knives and fire and many other risks to your health! There is no way I can stand by and see you get hurt," he'd said, and that was that.

Sheltered young ladies really do have it tough, huh…

Anyway, the point is that noble ladies didn't make their own food. So everything that was given to the council was made by professionals who were all artisans in their craft. With this in mind, it was natural for Maria to feel intimidated, being an amateur baker.

"While I do like artisan-crafted sweets, I also love homemade ones!"

"Oh...? Have you tried homemade sweets before, Lady Claes?" Maria asked, surprise written all over her face.

"Yes indeed. The head maid at my manor was very interested in baking. She'd often let me have some of her sweets."

While artisan-crafted sweets were surely as delicious as they looked, the simple, yet tasty treats that the head maid crafted were wonderful in their own way. In fact, I found myself pining for them now that I was no longer at the manor.

"And so you see, Miss Campbell... I find myself longing for those homemade treats now that I'm here at the academy! I'd love it if you could just give a small one to me when you bake another batch... Of course, I would pay for all your ingredients, and for the labor."

Oh, please, Maria. You simply have to give me some of those incredibly delicious sweets... I thought as I tried my best to smile sincerely with my villainess face. But would Maria be convinced? Would she understand my desperate struggle?

"No, no! That would not do at all, Lady Claes! There will be no expenses incurred, and even the ingredients are provided free by the academy's kitchens! It is merely a hobby of mine, and I have no way of knowing if my baking would suit your tastes... But I can definitely bring some for you in the near future..." Maria said, somewhat flustered.

"Really? Thank you very much!"

And so, I was able to secure the promise of Maria's wonderful homemade sweets.

The next day after classes, I walked alone back towards the dormitory to change into my overalls for field work.

Keith and the rest were currently in the council chambers, busy with council work. But I had received a special package today: the specially synthesized fertilizer Grandpa Tom made for me. I wanted to fertilize the fields as soon as possible, so I left the council chambers early.

This was why I was plodding step after step towards the dormitories, even though a familiar rumbling of protest emerged from my stomach. Of course, this was my own fault; I had forgotten to do some assignments before class this morning, so I'd borrowed Keith's notes, desperately copying them over breakfast. Naturally, I didn't eat much as I scribbled while listening to Keith's light scolding.

I suppose I could have Anne prepare something for me before I go out to the fields. As that thought flitted through my mind, I was jolted back to reality by my sense of smell. I could confidently say that my nose was like a dog's — and right now, a delicious aroma was floating through the air.

Before I knew it, I was stumbling towards the general direction of this sweet smell, and I soon found myself in a forested area slightly off the main path. Unexpectedly, I found Maria there, surrounded by what appeared to be some students from the academy.

From the look of their vibrant and fancy dresses, I supposed they were all noble ladies of high social standing. Maria was hugging to her chest a basket that had a handkerchief on top of it, hiding its contents. The smell that had called out to me was coming from that very basket.

So this means… No, it can't be! Could it be the homemade sweets I asked for yesterday? Wow, she made them by the very next day! She's so kind and generous!

Overcome with gratitude and emotion, I slowly started approaching the group... and that was when it happened. A loud slapping sound echoed through the forest.

One of the noble ladies surrounding Maria raised her hand and brought it down roughly on Maria's basket. The basket sailed for a short distance, before dropping onto the ground. Now lying on its side, several mini muffins rolled out from the fallen basket — Maria's homemade sweets.

"So what if you have Light Magic? Don't get full of yourself. Who do you think you are?! Look at this! Made by a commoner urchin like you! Don't you dare feed this to the student council! I won't allow such a disgusting thing!" the one who hit the basket said, before starting to...

Wait. Is she about to stomp on the sweets that Maria made?! SHE IS!

What are you doing?! Those are MY sweets!

"CEASE THIS AT ONCE!" I shouted, roughly cutting in between Maria and the other students.

"L-Lady Katarina... Claes..." said the student who was just about to step on the muffins, stuttering slightly. I could see all of their pupils dilate in fear at my sudden appearance.

"How *DARE* you?!" *These are sweets that Maria worked hard to bake! For me! MY sweets!* I glared angrily at the noble ladies before me.

"...E-Eek!" Almost immediately, the color faded from their faces. I did, after all, have the face of a villainess. And with me now glaring at them, the effect was probably multiplied several times over in intensity.

Sinners who have attempted to ruin my sweets... you will be eternally damned! I widened my eyes threateningly, turning an even more hostile gaze at the girls.

The noble ladies collectively felt my unbridled fury. "W-We're very sorry... do excuse us..." they said, bowing their heads and pale faces, before hurrying— no, dashing off in a fashion as elegant as possible for a noble lady.

...Hmph. I see that my villainess powers are doing as well as ever today. Even so... I turned to the sweets that had fallen onto the ground. Actually, the muffins had only rolled onto the grass of the lawn, and hadn't yet touched the dirt.

Kneeling down, I picked up the fallen basket and placed the sweets back into it. But as I did so, the smell of Maria's baked goods, still as delicious as ever, assaulted my empty stomach. Unable to bear with it any longer, I reached out towards the muffins in the basket... and popped a few of them into my mouth at once.

"...So good." They were incredibly delicious. In fact, they were some of the yummiest sweets I'd ever eaten.

These are just too good! They have such a delicate texture! They aren't too sweet, and they're so filling! The balance of flavor is just right — they're unbearably delicious!

The delectable taste of Maria's sweets overwhelmed me, and I soon found myself lost in their tasty goodness. Before I knew it, I had somehow emptied the entire basket... there wasn't a single morsel left.

With a satisfied expression, I sighed, only to see Maria staring at me with a mix of shock and disbelief on her face.

O-Oh no?! I got carried away again... How could I have eaten all of Maria's sweets?

Come to think of it, the basket was completely full. Maybe she meant to share them with the rest of the council...?

Actually... I ate them all thinking they were made for me, but... what if they were meant for someone else? This is bad... bad!

"Um... I'm sorry... It's a bad habit of mine, getting ahead of myself and eating everything up like that..." I apologized in a panic, bowing my head in Maria's general direction.

Maria responded by shrinking back a little, as if she had just seen something terrifying. "Ah, no... I don't mind, Lady Claes. It is just that... the sweets had fallen onto the ground..."

Oh. That's what she's concerned about. I was incredibly relieved. I don't know what I would have done if the sweets had been for someone else.

"They only fell onto the grass, Miss Campbell. They were mostly dirt-free. It's no problem, really." After all, I had picked them up right after and eaten them all. They were still under the five-second rule, so I issued my statement with utter confidence.

"...I-Is that so..." Maria replied, her smile obviously strained. Even so...

"You really are amazing, Miss Campbell. They were so delicious!" That was an understatement — the taste of Maria's homemade sweets had exceeded my expectations by far. They were truly delightful.

How it melts in one's mouth... the delicate balance of sweetness... Her skill could probably even match a professional patissier's.

In response to my impassioned praise…

"…Thank you very much…" Maria said, smiling shyly as she stood, her cheeks flushed. Just as I was about to lose myself in the lovely image, I caught sight of Jeord, who was approaching us from the direction of the school buildings.

Jeord had apparently decided to search for Maria, worried about how she had failed to turn up despite there being a meeting at the council today. Upon seeing me kneeling down with an empty basket and a red-faced Maria, he immediately regarded me with suspicion and surprise.

Maria, however, was quick to offer an explanation. "Ah, Prince Jeord… I coincidentally ran into Lady Katarina, who kindly spoke with me for a while…"

Thank you, Maria, for not saying something like, "Oh… Prince Jeord. Lady Claes ate all the sweets that I had prepared for the student council…"

If Jeord and Keith got wind of this, they would surely reprimand me, probably with something like *"To think that you would even eat sweets meant for others… have you no shame as a noble lady?"*

And so Jeord, having safely located Maria, whisked her away to the student council chambers. Of course, he tried to get me to come along too. But in the light of my impending field work and Grandpa Tom's special fertilizer, I politely declined.

With my stomach nicely filled, I headed back to the dormitories, changed into my overalls, and started walking off in the direction of the fields.

Still… I can't believe Maria would be bullied like that… This was what I kept thinking about as I repeatedly buried my hoe into the ground.

Maria Campbell was a commoner, blessed with the rare ability to wield Light Magic. She did well in school, and had a sweet face and personality. On top of all that, she was also a member of the student council, an organization adored by the students of this academy.

If anything, Maria should be the envy of the academy. Perhaps that was why those noble ladies bullied her; because of their jealousy and pride. That had to be why Maria was cornered by those students.

The antagonist of *Fortune Lover* was Katarina herself — she was the one who picked on the protagonist on a regular basis. But this pre-designated antagonist was now missing from the overall picture. Even so, there were plenty of prideful nobles at the academy. Even if Katarina wasn't there to lead them into bullying the protagonist, more of the same kind would appear anyway, just with different names and faces.

Those bullies were horrible in every way. How could they do such things to the sweets that Maria worked so hard to make? If I were a few seconds later, it would have been a complete disaster... the muffins would have been ruined!

Ugh! What horrible people! They're just like the Katarina in Fortune Lover! *With their silly pride and noses up in the air, bullying others... hmm? Katarina in...* Fortune Lover?

Hmm. Come to think of it... there was a scene like this in the game. Yes, one where Katarina bullies Maria, just like what I witnessed today... What exactly happened during that scene? Let's see...

Maria bakes sweets for everyone at the council, and is just headed that way when she is cornered by a group of sneering girls... who dash her creations into the ground, before stomping savagely on them.

The one who comes to her aid is Jeord, a potential love interest. Jeord would elegantly send all the bad nobles packing. He would then pick up one of the sweets on the ground and eat it. *"Most delicious, I must say,"* he would declare, smiling gently at Maria.

In fact, I remembered getting really excited at seeing Jeord's smile on the screen. It wasn't his stereotypical fake smile, but a truly genuine one.

I see... so today's events were that particular scene from the game? I hadn't noticed the similarities at the time, probably because the ringleader wasn't Katarina Claes. But the more I thought about it, the more sense it made — that was why Jeord had appeared right after the bullies had run off. After all, that encounter was one of Jeord's in-game events.

Ah, right. I see. So it was one of Jeord's events... Hmm? So... Wait. Does that mean that I snatched one of Jeord's events away from him?!

Wait. Under normal circumstances, Jeord was supposed to be the one who saved Maria... but instead, I intervened. The bad nobles were sent packing not by Prince Jeord, but me, the villainess-faced Katarina Claes... And I ended up eating all the sweets before Jeord got here — and so he never showed that gentle smile to Maria.

Oh... oh no. I'm really sorry, Jeord... How could I have stolen a romantic event from one of my important friends...? At this rate, Maria and Jeord's romance won't progress! I'm so sorry...

Hmm...? Actually, isn't that a good thing? After all, if Maria and Jeord get along too well, Katarina will be seen as an obstacle in the way of their true love, and eventually meet a Catastrophic Bad End...

Hmm. Then haven't I done well? Oh, yes I have! Good job, Katarina Claes! Turns out I played a part in avoiding a Bad End for myself, totally by coincidence!

Alright! I shall return to my tasks with renewed vigor! Filled with resolve, I started scattering the special fertilizer Grandpa Tom sent me, ensuring that it covered the field.

Unfortunately… I got a little too excited and scattered way too much. I had to ask Anne for help to gather it up, and I ended up working deep into the night and almost into dawn as I listened to Anne's scolding.

A few weeks passed since the incident where I accidentally replaced Jeord in one of his events. Ever since then, I found myself getting along much better with Maria, who had started baking sweets for me on a regular basis.

"Please help yourself, Lady Claes," Maria would say, smiling as she offered me a tray of those irresistibly delicious sweets. As a result, I often found my feet gravitating towards the council chambers.

If the other students knew about this, they'd definitely be filled with jealousy and hurl curses at me behind my back. After all, I was living a luxurious life — with Maria's delicious sweets and the student council president's amazing tea.

While Maria's sweets were in a class of their own, the president's tea was formidable too. You'd never think that he was the son of a noble, given how skilled he was. His tea always had a unique, smooth flavor to it.

Apparently the president and Nicol were distant relatives of some kind, and the two had met several times during their childhoods. This must have been why the president was armed with Nicol resistance.

It was surprising given his puppy-like looks and lovable personality, but the president was a really accomplished person. Nicol, being Chancellor Ascart's son, was impressive in his own right, but the president was beyond even him. He was top of his year in both academics and magic; definitely an extraordinary young man.

I was surprisingly charmed by the sight of him brewing tea with a faint smile on his face was charming, even though he was a year older than me. He was also impossibly fast at his tasks. He processed documents and forms on his desk at an unbelievable pace, all with that same serene smile. The difference between his work ethic and his calming presence was stark indeed.

Given that he was such a talented and likeable person, it was natural that he was popular with the student populace — same as my group of friends. He apparently had a fan club, too, who called themselves "The Devotees." I'd heard that the number of students in that club rivaled even Nicol's fans. That made me wonder if the students who'd been in the council last year were only bewitched by Nicol.

In the original setting of *Fortune Lover*, the president only played a minor role, and hardly had much screen time. But seeing him now, I thought it would make sense if he were a potential love interest.

That beloved president was now pouring tea for me, and constantly refilling my cup as soon as I asked… If the other students found out about this, they would seethe with envy. I suddenly felt very grateful for the fact the council chambers were off limits to all except council members.

I got along well with other council members aside from my friends, but I didn't have much contact with them outside of the chambers. The president was a year older, so he was in different classes. But Maria was in the same year as I was, and naturally took the same lessons as I did.

I thought we would get along even outside the council, but I couldn't help but notice that Maria stayed at a distance while we were outside the chambers. I supposed it was due to the social standing of me and my friends, since we stood at the pinnacle of noble society. And it wasn't only Maria — most other students avoided me too. Almost no one outside my rank was friendly towards me.

In fact, Maria herself faced a similar problem in the original setting of *Fortune Lover* — her potential love interests hardly interacted with her much outside of the student council chamber. As the player progressed and scored points with the relevant love interest, they would become fond of Maria, and eventually spend time with her even outside of council activities.

At this point in time, however, it seemed like Maria didn't have much in the way of potential love interests at all. Although everyone was friendly to her, no one seemed to be particularly smitten. Actually since I'd become a slave to Maria's perfectly balanced sweets, if there was anyone who would be smitten with Maria, it was *me*.

With how things were, no one else in the council seemed interested in approaching Maria very much at all. In fact, she probably spent most of her time outside of the council alone. It was during these times that she was bullied by Katarina in the game's setting, and now, others with similar intentions were filling that role.

I felt like I should do something about it. With that in mind, I approached Keith, my wise brother. Keith had a simple, but effective idea: that Maria should simply stay with us outside of council hours. After all, we came from the pinnacle of this kingdom's noble society. Keith reasoned that if Maria stayed close to us, even the most highly ranked nobles in the academy wouldn't be able to bother her.

When I found myself panicking, having forgotten to do some assignments for one lecture or another, it was Maria who lent me her easily understandable notes. She even patiently explained all the theories and concepts to me. And when I begged her to, it was Maria who took the effort to bake delicious sweets for me, and then served them to me on a tray with a warm smile.

Before I knew it, I had become very fond of Maria Campbell — the protagonist who was originally the arch-enemy of the antagonist Katarina Claes. This was why I couldn't ignore the things that were happening to her. I couldn't simply avert my eyes and pretend she was not suffering.

Alright! I'm not gonna wait for the love interest to latch onto Maria, since they've been so slow this whole time!

I'll do everything I can to close the distance between Maria and I, so that we can be friends and have fun outside the council chamber's walls!

It happened a few days after I had made up my mind and steeled my resolve. I found myself searching for Maria during a lunch break, thinking that this was the day when I would invite her to have lunch with me.

My friends and I usually ate in the dining hall during lunch break, but I had never seen Maria there. I had read in the script of *Fortune Lover* that Maria felt intimidated by the sheer number of nobles in the dining hall, and as a result, returned to her dormitory to prepare her meals and then ate somewhere else.

With that information in hand, I searched the grounds for a place where someone could eat a meal and soon came across Maria, seated on a solitary bench on the fringes of the academy's courtyard.

But Maria wasn't alone. She was surrounded again by the same noble ladies that had bullied her several weeks ago. While there was still some distance between us, I could hear the nobles somewhat clearly, their voices carried by the wind.

"You filthy commoner! Just because you have some Light Magic, you got selected for the council! Don't get ahead of yourself!"

"You get special treatment because of that silly Light Magic of yours, don't you? They had no choice but to put you on the council! Simply disgusting!"

"That's right! You probably just got preferential treatment in your student evaluation tests! It has to be that!"

The noble ladies surrounding Maria pelted her with verbal abuse. Amidst all that, one of them raised her hand high — and from her palm, a red, flickering glow appeared.

That's… Fire Magic! She's going to hurt Maria with it..! My feet sprang to life. I had to close the distance between Maria and the fire-handed student. *Maria is in real danger! But… I'm still too far! There's too much distance between us… if it's come to this…*

"COME FORTH! DIRT BUMP!" I shouted at the top of my lungs. At my command, an earthen wall about ten centimeters in height rose up between Maria and the fire-handed noble lady who had been relentlessly approaching her target.

And of course, she then tripped and landed spectacularly on her behind.

ALRIGHT! I thought, visualizing myself standing in place with a flex-pose. *Behold, the power of my Dirt Bump, honed through long years of practice and training!*

With their leader now fumbling around on the ground, the group of bullies seemed confused and alarmed. Not letting this opportunity go to waste, I sprinted towards Maria and placed myself between her and the bullies.

Turning to the nobles, I glared at them with my villainess face. "How DARE you say such a thing?! That she gets preferential treatment because of Light Magic... that's a bunch of crap! This academy rewards people based on merit!"

After all, if there were any preferential treatment at the academy, there was no way the daughter of a duke would have such mediocre grades.

"You also got one thing wrong... Maria is a hard worker! That's why she scored well! Because she gave it her all!"

And that was exactly right. While I'd thought that Maria was some kind of invincible genius when I played *Fortune Lover*, in reality, Maria was hardworking and earnest. When I forgot to do my assignments or take notes, she showed me her textbook and taught me what I needed to know. From the detail of her notes, it was plain to see that Maria worked hard on a daily basis. Maria was no genius — she simply put in all her effort.

"Also... the student council and me? We don't stand with her because she wields Light Magic! We do because she tries harder than anyone else... and that's why we're on her side! Because we LIKE her!" I declared, continuing to stare at the bullies with my villainess glare.

Then, I allowed an evil smile to creep into the corners of my lips. "You all... If you dare keep this up... I'll see to it that you meet a... *Bad End*."

Yes — a Catastrophic Bad End — just like the original Katarina Claes. And with that, the noble ladies, perhaps having felt true fear upon seeing my ultimate villainess death glare, bolted off in unison, dashing away as ladylike a fashion as possible.

Hmph. What a spineless bunch. Small fries like that cannot possibly hope to stand up to the force of nature that is antagonist villainess extraordinaire — Katarina Claes! BWA HA HA HA HA! I found myself mentally laughing wickedly.

And so, I ended up using the villainous features of Katarina Claes to great success. Having chased away the malicious nobles, I turned back to Maria, only to find...

What...?! Is she c-crying?!

"M-Maria?!" Panicking, I approached Maria, placing a hand on her shivering back. *She must have been scared... being surrounded like that, and threatened with magic... She must have been so scared.*

I slowly rubbed Maria's back, attempting to soothe her. For a while, we remained like that, with my hand still moving in circles, until the silence was broken by Maria.

"Ah... Um... Lady Claes, my name..."

Hmm? Name? What's she talking about? I thought about it for a second until the answer flitted into my mind. *Ah, come to think of it, I ended up calling her "Maria." Up until now I'd always called her "Miss Campbell"...*

"Ah, yes... about that. I apologize, suddenly acting like we're close friends..."

Maria shook her head to dismiss my panicked concerns. "No… I do not mind at all. In fact, there is no need to be formal. Please just call me 'Maria'…" she said earnestly.

Overwhelmed by how sweet she was, I found myself calling her name without a second thought. "Thank you, Maria." For some reason, I felt like we were now suddenly much closer.

Maria's smile seemed to light up her blushing face. "Ah… Um. I-If… you would forgive my impudence for…" She seemed to be acting a little strangely. In fact, she was now staring intently at me. "Um… Could I please call you 'Lady Katarina,' just like everyone else on the student council…?" she asked, her words carrying as much weight as a confession of love.

Once again, I felt my heart involuntarily skip a beat. "Of course! Feel free to call me whatever you like, Maria. After all, are we not already friends?" I said with my best smile.

While Maria's tears had almost all dried up mere moments ago, they were now streaming down her face once more. Again, I found myself desperately attempting to comfort her.

After quite some time, Maria finally calmed down. Then, as if on cue, Keith appeared from behind some trees. He had apparently been searching for me since I didn't show up at the dining hall.

The three of us ended up going there together, whereupon I wolfed down my lunch as quickly as I could in the company of my friends. Maria even shared a little of her homemade lunch with me — and it was truly delicious, just like her sweets were.

Ever since that day, Maria and I began to spend time together even outside of the council, and we became good friends.

But... I can't believe what I saw. Threatening another person with magic like that... unbelievable...

I couldn't stop thinking about it as I lay in my bed at the end of the day. The thought of it made me shiver. If I hadn't stopped that student there and then, and she had turned her flames on Maria... I was sure she would have been hurt, at the very least.

Threatening another person with magic like that is a crime. If that girl kept it up, she would definitely be exiled from the country or worse — just like Katarina Claes in *Fortune Lover.*

...Come to think of it, Katarina herself did similar things during my playthrough of the game. For some reason, something about that memory made me crawl out of bed. I reached for some papers that I hadn't read in a long while.

These were the collection of documents that I had written once I realized that this was the world of *Fortune Lover.* It contained memories of my past life, as well as information on the game. I called it the "*Fortune Lover* Unofficial Strategy Guide."

I was searching for a very specific thing: information on a certain event...

One afternoon, Katarina and her groupies surround Maria, as usual. After peppering Maria with a seemingly endless stream of verbal abuse, one of Katarina's flunkies summons a ball of flame into her palm, motioning to hurt Maria with it.

Just as the flames are about to strike her, Maria feels her entire body lifted upwards — and finds herself in the embrace of an earthen golem. The golem is several times bigger than the average person, and it seems to be protecting her.

This particular sort of magic is that of Keith Claes, who just so happened to be nearby. Keith's earthen golem carries Maria off to safety, eventually returning to where he's waiting a short distance away.

The reason why Keith himself didn't intervene was that the leader of the bullies was his adoptive sister, Katarina Claes. So he wanted to keep from showing his face and causing trouble.

Upon being lowered to safety, Maria bursts into tears, terrified and traumatized by the encounter. Keith, in turn, would gently comfort Maria as he held her in a somewhat awkward hug.

Given that he was usually a playboy, seeing Keith hug Maria in such a hesitant fashion was *so* cute. At least, from the player's perspective...

Hmm. So... I did it again?! I ended up stealing someone else's event again! And to make things worse, it was one of Keith's!

What have I done?! I even swore that I wouldn't interfere with his affairs in love and courtship, but I went ahead and stole one of his events! Oh, my dear brother... I am so sorry.

With this... Maria and Keith's romance may never develop in the first place. Ah, I am truly sorry, Keith... but. Hmm. Actually... isn't this actually a good thing? After all, if Keith falls in love with Maria, Katarina would become an obstacle, and hence meet a Catastrophic Bad End...

Hmm. Actually, well done, Katarina! You're great!

I've coincidentally dodged yet another Bad End, just like the time with Jeord! Ah, this is wonderful. I never knew I was so clever!

And so I continued showering myself with praise, and eventually fell asleep in a great mood.

The one significant takeaway from this event was that I became a lot closer with the protagonist, Maria Campbell. This was a huge advantage, because I was now able to check in on Maria's love life.

Naturally, now that Maria and I were close friends, questions like "So... do you have someone you like? Who is it?" would be totally normal in a gathering of girls. Determining the object of Maria's affections would be easy as pie!

...Or so I thought.

Unfortunately, my grand plan didn't quite work as well as I had intended it to. When I casually asked Maria, "Hey, Maria... Do you have someone you like?"

"I... I really admire and respect *you*, Lady Katarina..." Maria said, her cheeks flushed a deep shade of red.

Well... that's very kind of you to say, Maria, but that's not what I meant...

On top of that, Maria's response immediately drew similar declarations from my childhood friends, Mary and Sophia.

"Me too, me too! I admire Lady Katarina more than anyone... More than anyone!"

"You c-can't have her all to yourselves... Lady Maria, Lady Mary! M-Me too... I admire you too, Lady Katarina...!"

They each chimed in like this. *Ah, I really do have such amazing friends. But... I wanted to speak of romantic love, not friendship...*

After that, our little group stopped talking about love interests altogether, and the conversation was derailed into some sort of Katarina-praising contest.

While I did feel honored to be spoken of like that, I couldn't find out anything about Maria's love interest... and time slowly passed us by. But alas... few things go according to plan in life.

As I got closer to Maria, I realized that there was another layer to her charm. For instance… the delicious sweets that Maria baked seemed to be tailor-made to my tastes. And she'd also take very easy-to-understand, gently annotated lecture notes for me. And then there was how she would sometimes smile shyly when our eyes met, with that lovely, faint smile of hers.

If I were a man, I would have already been hopelessly smitten. I had only accidentally taken some events for myself, and yet, I felt powerless in the face of Maria's overwhelming charm and lovability. It was easy to understand why all the love interests in *Fortune Lover* fell for her so quickly.

Now that I had a deeper friendship with her, I couldn't help but feel an impending sense of danger, caused by Maria's impossibly powerful charms.

"So… how did that feel? Was that natural at all?" I asked, only for Anne to raise an eyebrow in response.

"…Do excuse me, young miss. But what exactly… what exactly is this?"

"What do you mean, Anne? Don't you see? I'm practicing tossing my projectile snake toy in the most natural way possible!"

Ah, you can be so silly sometimes, Anne. I already explained it several times before I began…

"…Yes, it is as you say, young miss. You did, in fact, inform me about this… practice of yours several times. However… I still do not quite understand what purpose this practice serves…"

"But I already told you all about it, Anne! In case it's ever necessary, I need to be able to momentarily frighten my opponent… and create an opening for myself!"

"...Young miss. I... I am sorry, but I do not understand this 'ever necessary' moment that you are speaking of..."

"Oh, you know, when things come down to it! Quickly now, I'm going to toss it again, please tell me how natural it looks..." I returned the snake to my pocket, before once again practicing the motion of my throw.

"To begin with... I hardly think that tossing a snake toy from one's pocket is natural behavior of any order..." Anne seemed to be mumbling something under her breath — her words didn't reach me, however, as I was engrossed in perfecting my snake toy toss.

And so I continued practicing and perfecting my projectile snake toy throwing, all for the sake of avoiding a Catastrophic Bad End at the hands of one who had fallen for Maria's irresistible charms.

Meanwhile, I also managed to widen the fields a little — more crops on the horizon!

★★★★★★★★★★

My name is Maria Campbell. However, few people call me by that name. Everyone calls me this instead: "The special child, Wielder of Light Magic."

I was born and raised in a small town a short distance away from the kingdom's capital... and I was only five when my Light Magic manifested.

A friend who had been playing with me tripped and fell, hurting her leg in the process. The open wound on her skin looked like it really, really hurt. *If only I could help heal it,* I thought. So I touched the wound ever so slightly.

And with that, a bright, dazzling light erupted from my hand. The wound that I was touching started to close before my eyes. Light Magic was the magic of healing, or curing illnesses and injuries. However, I knew little of such things at the time.

Had I been born to a noble family, I would have had the opportunity to study magic. But I was born to a common family. At the time I hadn't yet even started attending school, and so there was no way I could have known anything about magic.

The friend whom I had healed with my light was the same. All I did was stick my hand out — and then there was a bright light… and then the wound was gone.

She seemed surprised, then afraid. My friend screamed, before pushing me away and fleeing. In my confusion, all I could do was sit in place until my mother eventually came looking for me.

Quite some time passed before I told my mother the truth of the incident. As soon as I had done so, however, I was dragged to the town's public office, where I was subjected to examinations.

The results were clear — I was soon designated as "a potential Wielder of Light."

Before my magical abilities manifested, I was a common child, the same as any other. My family wasn't especially wealthy. My father was courageous and dependable, while my mother was gentle, and loved baking in her spare time. I lived happily with my parents.

If there was ever anything special about me, it would be the beauty of my kind mother. She was said to be the most beautiful woman in the town. I mostly took after my mother, and was well-loved by my father, and all my fellow townsfolk.

However... that all changed when my "Light Magic" manifested. Most magic-users in the kingdom were of noble descent. Cases in which commoners had magical capabilities were exceedingly rare.

Rare as said cases may be, they were still possible — although most of such children were born of affairs, the child of a commoner with a single noble parent. As a result, when my magical capabilities came to light... my mother was suspected of being unfaithful. Perhaps it was because I took after my mother too much, and hardly had any of my father's traits.

My mother's beauty hardly helped... and soon the rumors began to swirl that she'd had an affair with a nobleman somewhere. My mother did no such thing, but rumors spread quickly in small towns like ours. Our familial bonds suffered immeasurably as a result.

Eventually, my father, who would always come home immediately after work to speak to my mother and I, stopped coming home at all. My gentle and kind mother, who had always smiled, was now expressionless, her eyes permanently downcast. Although she had loved baking cookies and cakes before, she suddenly stopped. All because of my magic.

The changes didn't end there, however... The townsfolk, who were all kind to me before, now kept me at arm's length. The friends that I used to get along with so well no longer wanted to play with me. People suspected me of being the illegitimate child of a noble somewhere, or a strange, abnormal child with magical capabilities. I was now a presence that the people of this small town could not easily accept...

Everyone regarded me with awe. They never approached me, they were afraid of me, and they went to extreme lengths to avoid me — all because of my Light Magic.

Even so… I couldn't simply give up, not even when faced with all these things that were out of my control. I wanted my father to come home… I wanted my mother to smile again… and I wanted to play with my friends.

And so I worked hard… I helped out with the chores as much as I could. I never said anything selfish or demanded anything for myself, and I desperately threw myself into my studies.

After all… if I tried really hard, if I was good and did the right things, I believed that one day, everything would go back to how it used to be. I would have my happy life back.

Before I knew it, everyone started regarding me with a sort of silent, but distant awe. "Maria Campbell is a special child," they would say. I had started going to a nearby school, and scored high grades in my studies there. The teachers praised me.

However… nothing changed. My father did not come home, and my mother's gaze remained downcast. Although the other children didn't exactly ignore me or bully me, no one wanted to play with me. No matter how hard I tried, no matter how many people called me "special"… nothing changed.

Eventually, those around me started whispering… "Because she's the illegitimate child of a noble, they let her cheat…" or "She's just tricking them all with her magic…"

What do I have to do to get along with everyone? That was the thought that was always on my mind.

One day, a female classmate of mine brought some homemade treats to class. All my classmates happily ate them. *If I made treats for everyone like that girl did, would I get along with everyone better?*

Before my magic manifested, I often made sweets with my mother. The sweets that I had baked with her were very, very delicious. After I returned home that day, I started to recall the steps that my mother had taught me, and for the first time in my life, started baking myself.

With quite some effort, I finally completed my endeavor. Although they didn't taste as good as the ones I had made with my mother back then, they still had a very nostalgic taste. They filled my heart with warmth.

And so I kept practicing, again and again, until I was finally confident in how they tasted. Then I brought my sweets to school…

And just like my classmate had done before, I laid out my sweets on the lunchroom table that all of my classmates were seated at. However… not a single one was eaten by any of my classmates. Not a single hand reached out to them.

At the end of our lunch break, everyone returned to their seats. I packed up the uneaten sweets, placing them into my bag. Class ended, and all my classmates left and went home, leaving me alone in the classroom.

I took a single snack out of my bag, and put it into my mouth. Although I was usually cheered up when snacking on treats like this, now I was crying instead. I didn't understand why the tears wouldn't stop, as drop after drop fell from my cheeks.

I continued crying as I ate, snack after snack, treat after treat. Eventually, I finished them all. Once I got home, I immediately crawled into bed.

"Aren't you going to have dinner?" my mother asked in a monotone voice from beyond the door to my room. It was as if taking care of me was only some sort of obligation.

"I am not hungry today," I said.

My mother's response was as monotonous as ever. "I see," she said, and walked away.

The teachers in my school, my classmates, the people in town, and now my family... everyone called me "special." But that "special" meant that I was abnormal. No matter how hard I tried, no matter what I did, I would always be kept at arm's length and regarded with fear.

I don't want them to call me that anymore... I don't want to be called a "special child who wields Light Magic" anymore!

I'm not some illegitimate child of a noble! I've never cheated with my magic...! All I've done is work hard so that everyone would accept me! I... I only did my best...

No one would look at me. Even my mother averted her eyes. *Anyone... please. Anyone is fine... please, just... look at me! Look at Maria Campbell!*

The law of the land stated that all those who had magical capability had to attend the Academy of Magic once they came of age at fifteen.

The Academy of Magic... surely all the students there will have magic of some kind. Maybe I can just be a normal child there. If I go to the academy... maybe I'll be able to make friends.

That was what I thought to myself as I curled up on my bed, in my dark, lonely room. Slowly but surely, hope sprung from the depths of my heart.

If I go to the Academy of Magic...

And so, with the hope that I had nurtured in my heart all this time, I went to the academy… only for that hope to be shattered even sooner than I expected.

The students of the academy were all children of nobility — the very existence of a commoner like me was an abnormality. To make things worse, the unusual nature of Light Magic was known even amongst the common folk, so I knew that I was a rarity even amongst those who did have magic.

As a result, I only continued to stand out. More and more factors made me abnormal and strange, and I soon realized that I would not be making any friends. In fact, I was soon bullied for having Light Magic "despite being a commoner." Apparently, it was seen as a gesture of arrogance.

Little changed at the academy. Things were just how they were back when I lived in my hometown. It was difficult just to get through the day. However… I thought that if I tried my best, if I did the right things and was a good person… then surely things would change. So I continued working hard.

A few weeks after starting at the academy, the student academic and magical aptitude tests took place. I suppose there was some value to all the hard work I had put in, as I achieved good grades on those tests. As a result, I ended up becoming part of the student council.

The other members of the council were of high social standing. These were people whom I would not ever speak with had I lived in that town all my life. Our second-year seniors were socially important people too. Surrounded by such individuals, I couldn't help but act reserved.

But it didn't take me long to realize that these people hardly thought about social station or position. They were all kind and friendly, never putting on airs.

In particular, there was one person who was particularly kind — a certain Lady Katarina Claes, the daughter of Duke Claes. For some reason, she was well-loved by most of the other council members, and an exception was made to allow her into the council chambers even though she was not a formal member. She treated everyone the same way, be they noble or commoner. Lady Katarina Claes was always gentle and warm.

The student council chambers soon became the only place in the academy where I could rest my heart and soul.

"Would you be interested in baking some sweets and bringing them here to share with us, Miss Campbell?"

One day after lessons, Lady Katarina asked such a question. It was all so sudden — I found myself freezing in place.

"...Um. Lady Claes... how is it that you know about my baking...?"

It was true, however, that I had continued baking ever since that incident. My mother's recipe reminded me of the past. I always felt a little better after eating those baked sweets. Even though I had faced hardship and difficulty ever since coming to the academy, I still continued baking, borrowing a small corner of the kitchens to do so.

However, I had done all of this in secret, and I had never spoken to anyone on the student council about it. So why did Lady Katarina know about this? I looked at her with confusion.

"Umm... Uh. Th-That was... because I heard about it from the chefs of the dining hall, so..." Lady Katarina replied.

While it was true that I had asked the chefs to keep it secret, it was possible that rumors of my activities had leaked out one way or another. So I admitted that it was true, but I quickly said, "The baked goods I make are hardly worthy of the palates of those on the council, so..."

I looked at the delicately crafted sweets laid out on the table. I had never seen such expensive-looking sweets in all my life, but the council ate them on a regular basis. *I could never present my cheap-looking, homemade sweets next to them,* I thought, withdrawing into myself.

"While I do like artisan-crafted sweets, I also love homemade ones!" Lady Katarina said.

I was surprised, and asked if she had ever had homemade sweets. After all, the nobility of this kingdom hardly did any work in the kitchens. As a result, everything they ate was crafted by artisans and professional chefs. I had assumed that nobles would never eat anything that was homemade by amateurs.

Lady Katarina told me that the head maid at her manor had baked sweets for her. Then, smiling charmingly, she said, "And so you see, Miss Campbell... I find myself longing for those homemade treats now that I'm here at the academy! I'd love it if you could just give a small one to me when you bake another batch... Of course, I would pay for all your ingredients, and for the labor."

"No, no! That would not do at all, Lady Claes! There will be no expenses incurred, and even the ingredients are provided free by the academy's kitchens! It is merely a hobby of mine, and I have no way of knowing if my baking would suit your tastes... But I can definitely bring some for you in the near future..."

Even though I knew that my sweets were hardly worthy of being eaten by a noble like Lady Katarina, I found myself agreeing, pulled in by her smile. And then, to someone like me...

"Really? Thank you very much!" Lady Katarina said, once again giving me that charming smile.

Perhaps Lady Katarina was speaking out of pity. I was a commoner, and was always alone... baking sweets in a small corner of the kitchens. Maybe she had heard the rumors that I had eaten all those sweets by myself, and had asked to try some out of sympathy for my situation.

However... Lady Katarina was a very gentle and kind person. Even if this was about sympathy, pity, or just social formalities, it was the first time that anyone had asked to taste the sweets that I made.

I found myself in a buoyant mood. Immediately after returning to the dormitories, I prepared my tools, and then went to the kitchens that very night to bake the sweets Lady Katarina had requested. This was the first time I would be baking for anyone else — ever since the time I cried and ate alone.

The next day, I headed to the dormitory's dining hall before going to the student council chambers. I warmed up the sweets I had left in the kitchens slightly to try to make them as enjoyable as possible for Lady Katarina.

And so, with my basket full of warmed treats, I headed in the direction of the council chambers... and that was when it happened.

On my way to the school buildings from the dormitories, I was stopped by several female students. From the look of their expensive, vibrantly colored dresses, I could tell that they were high-ranking noble ladies.

"We have some matters to discuss."

With that, the group forcefully escorted me to a nearby forested area. Once we were away from the path, the noble ladies started yelling at me, hurling verbal abuse of all kinds and calling me a filthy commoner.

This had happened many times ever since I had started at the academy. I kept my eyes downcast, staring at the ground, hoping that the noble ladies would eventually calm down and leave. However...

"And what is this?" one of the noble ladies said, pointing to the basket I was holding to my chest.

"...Ah... this... these are just some sweets I made, as a gift for the student council..." I found myself answering truthfully out of surprise at being abruptly questioned. I soon regretted my clumsiness in doing so, however.

Upon hearing my answer, the noble ladies' expressions collectively changed. While their faces were flushed red with anger before, they now seemed even more upset. They were furious.

Now I've done it... My careless words had agitated the noble ladies even further. And then — with a loud crack, the basket that I was holding was brutally slapped out of my hands, falling roughly onto the ground. The freshly warmed muffins rolled out of the fallen basket and then came to a stop on the grassy ground.

"So what if you have Light Magic? Don't get full of yourself. Who do you think you are?! Look at this! Made by a commoner urchin like you! Don't you dare feed this to the student council! I won't allow such a disgusting thing!" the noble lady screamed, before raising her foot in preparation to crush the fallen sweets.

I had never felt such anger directed at me before. Nothing I had felt in my life could compare to this. I could only stand, dumbstruck, as I stared at what was about to unfold before me.

But then…

"CEASE THIS AT ONCE!" A sudden voice, ringing out in the air. It was confident and dignified. With her long brown hair and azure eyes, her appearance was as dignified as her voice.

Why would she be here, of all places? Wasn't she always at the council chambers after lessons…? This person placed herself between me and the noble ladies, as if to shield me from their anger.

"L-Lady Katarina… Claes…" the noble lady who was about to step on my sweets muttered in shock. Although I was stunned at this turn of events, it seemed that the nobles who surrounded me were even more taken aback. Their eyes were open wide.

"How *DARE* you?!"

All the color drained from their faces at Lady Katarina's harsh inquiry. But of course they would feel that way… Lady Katarina Claes was the daughter of Duke Claes, and also the fiancée of the third prince of the kingdom, Prince Jeord. The student council, which was admired by the student populace, adored Lady Katarina. In fact, her bright and personable nature was secretly admired by many anonymous individuals in the academy.

If one were to upset Lady Katarina Claes, not only would they find it difficult to live on in the academy — they would also find themselves hard-pressed to remain in the kingdom at all.

And before I knew it, all those noble ladies who were so angry before were now impossibly meek and quiet. They apologized and bowed to Lady Katarina, and then, as if engaged in a fierce competition with one another, ran away as quickly as they could from where we stood.

All I could do was stare on quietly in the light of this sudden development... until I realized that I had to quickly make my way to the council chambers. I had to bring my treats to the council... But then I remembered that my sweets were no longer in my arms, but instead were scattered on the ground.

Ah... I can't possibly bring them to the council chambers now. I felt an old memory resurfacing in my mind, one of a time when no one would eat the treats I had baked. About how they were left on the table, untouched, even though I had worked so hard to make them. No one would even reach for them.

Still rooted to the spot, I watched as Lady Katarina knelt down, slowly picking up and returning the fallen sweets to the basket. But this made me panic. How could I let Lady Katarina pick up fallen objects from the ground? As I was about to raise an objection, Lady Katarina opened her mouth wide, and then promptly placed a snack into her mouth. And then —

"...So good," she said, smiling gently.

Sweets that had fallen onto the ground... I had thought that I would have to eat them all by myself, just like I did back then — but there she was. Lady Katarina was eating the muffins I had baked. She was saying they were delicious, and smiling.

The sight was too much for me to bear. I could only stare at Lady Katarina with wide eyes. Before long, she had eaten every last muffin. I met her gaze, and her azure-blue eyes stared deep into mine.

Lady Katarina then apologized for getting ahead of herself and eating them up, bowing her head. But... I couldn't even begin to understand why she would apologize.

"Ah, no... I don't mind, Lady Claes. It is just that... the sweets had fallen onto the ground..."

Lady Katarina, however, had a confident look about her as she responded. "They only fell onto the grass, Miss Campbell. They were mostly dirt-free. It's no problem, really."

I no longer knew how to respond to what I had just heard. All I could do was muster a strange smile. "...I-Is that so..."

Lady Katarina then went on to earnestly, fervently praise the sweets I had made. I had never been praised like this before. I felt so happy, but yet so embarrassed, that I could feel my face heating up.

It was then that Prince Jeord came along from the direction of the student council chambers. He had apparently come to look for me, on account of my being late for the meeting we were supposed to have.

Prince Jeord, however, looked at Lady Katarina suspiciously — she was hugging the basket close to her chest, still kneeling down on the ground, and my face was a deep shade of red. I came up with the best explanation I could, telling him that we had run into each other and were talking.

I didn't want to tell the prince about the bullying. It would be unbecoming for the council to worry about me. As if understanding how I felt, Prince Jeord turned to Lady Katarina, and soon we were all walking together.

On our way to the council chambers, I could still feel my flushed cheeks. Prince Jeord turned to me with an indecipherable smile on his face. "You should be careful, Miss Campbell. She is quite the charmer, you see." I didn't quite understand what he meant.

Ever since that day, I made sweets for the council on an almost daily basis. Lady Katarina, for her part, seemed very happy at this development.

It didn't take me long to notice that the bullying and gossip seemed to decrease after the incident in which Lady Katarina shielded me — and hence, I let my guard down. It was then that it happened… on the lunch break of a certain day.

The dining hall in the academy was a grand and respectable structure, and was regularly patronized by nobles of all kinds. With the academy itself having many students of noble birth, it goes without saying that many of them chose to have their meals there.

Just like how we were segregated into different dormitories by social status, seats in the dining hall were also split up in such a way. Being a commoner myself, however, there didn't seem to be a place for me. After all, there was only one eating area in the academy… and it was mostly filled with noble students of high social standing.

I was far from being able to use the dining hall myself, being all too aware of my own status as a mere commoner. This was why I often prepared lunch boxes in my dormitory room, and then had my meals alone somewhere in the academy's central courtyard.

That day was like any other — I sat down on a small bench in the courtyard, just like I always did, and was about to open up my lunch box. And then, before I knew it, I was once again surrounded by noble ladies I did not recall crossing paths with before.

They began to pepper me with verbal abuse, saying that I was given preferential treatment because of my Light Magic. They said that the only reason I attained high scores on the evaluation tests was because of this.

I kept quiet, just like I always did, waiting for their fury to subside. Their words were the very same words that I had heard ever since I came to the academy… no, I had heard them ever since the beginning of it all.

"Because you wield Light Magic." Those were the words that had plagued me ever since my magic manifested itself. No matter how hard I worked, or how hard I tried… it would all be because I could use Light Magic. That was all anyone would say.

If they want it so badly… if I could just give it away to someone. I would do it in a heartbeat… I don't need this… I don't need this at all! I just… I just!

While I was lost in my thoughts and an unending torrent of abuse, one of the noble ladies raised her hand — and in her palm was a ball of flame, burning bright and red.

Up until now, I had been slapped in the face countless times, stomped on the foot more times than I could remember, and was regularly bullied in all sorts of ways. But… magic like this was a first. I stared at the red-hot ball of fire. It didn't feel real to me — all I could do was stare at it, as if it were some otherworldly object.

Just as the bully took a step forward, the flames in her hand raised high. I thought I heard a clear voice ring out, and then, without warning, the bully who had been approaching me menacingly all this while fell on her behind right before my eyes. Before I could even react, a familiar dignified silhouette entered my field of vision.

""How DARE you say such a thing?! That she gets preferential treatment because of Light Magic… that's a bunch of crap! This academy rewards people based on merit! You also got one thing wrong… Maria is a hard worker! That's why she scored well! Because she gave it her all!"

Shielding me from the bullies once again was Lady Katarina Claes.

Yes. It was just as Lady Katarina said. I'd always worked hard. I never cheated on my tests, either. All I did was try my best. And yet, no one noticed my efforts… or so I thought. In spite of everything, this person had noticed. I opened my eyes wide and stared straight into Lady Katarina's back.

As I continued staring, dumbstruck, she continued, "Also... the student council and me? We don't stand with her because she wields Light Magic! We do because she tries harder than anyone else... and that's why we're on her side! Because we LIKE her!"

At her words, I felt my eyes getting hot. Before long, tears were streaming down my cheeks. Ever since the day my magic had manifested, everyone had said I was special, but they had treated me like an abnormality. No matter how hard I worked or how much I tried, my efforts would simply be dismissed. All because I had this "special power," or perhaps because I cheated. Everyone saw me as "the special child who wielded Light Magic." No one would ever see me as Maria Campbell — just a human being, just a girl.

Even so... Lady Katarina... she noticed. She noticed that I tried hard. And she liked me not because I was some special child with Light Magic, but because I was Maria Campbell. And with that, I felt a wave of emotions well up within me and spill forth. It was as if a dam had burst open deep in my heart. The tears simply would not stop flowing.

Lady Katarina approached me as I continued crying, before placing a hand on my back. The gentle warmth of her hand caused the question in my heart to leave my lips before I even noticed it.

"Ah... Um... Lady Claes, my name..." Lady Katarina always referred to me as "Miss Campbell." But just now, as she was reprimanding the bullies, she had called me by my first name — "Maria."

Lady Katarina apologized, looking flustered, but I shook my head vigorously from side to side. "No... I do not mind at all. In fact, there is no need to be formal. Please just call me 'Maria'..."

Lady Katarina simply smiled gently at my request. "Thank you, Maria."

Upon hearing her distinguished voice call out my name, I mustered up all the courage in my being. "Ah... Um. I-If... you would forgive my impudence for... Um... Could I please call you 'Lady Katarina,' just like everyone else on the student council...?" I said, desperately asking the question I had in my heart.

Lady Katarina seemed momentarily stunned, but then... "Of course! Feel free to call me whatever you like, Maria. After all, are we not already friends?" she said, with that same gentle smile on her face.

To think that she, a noble, would call a commoner like me, a friend... I found myself crying once more, just when I had finally calmed down.

Anyone... please. Anyone is fine... please, just... look at me! Look at Maria Campbell... That was what I had always wished for. If I worked harder... if I go to the Academy of Magic, then...

With each and every hope I had cradled in my heart cruelly dashed to pieces, I had thought that my wish would never come true — and yet

Tears continued flowing down my cheeks as Lady Katarina's warm hand gently moved across my back. I was so happy that my dream had finally been fulfilled... And for a while, we sat like that. I eventually calmed down, and Master Keith came by to pick Lady Katarina up. The three of us then headed to the dining hall...

I found myself blushing as Lady Katarina held her hand out to me. Upon seeing this, Master Keith sighed, as if exasperated. "... Again?! Just how many people must you charm...?"

I wonder what Master Keith meant.

Ever since then, I became closer with Lady Katarina and her friends, even outside of our activities at the student council. We took classes together, and after our lessons, we all headed straight to the student council chambers.

When I took out the sweets that I had baked for the council, Lady Katarina was overjoyed. I was glad too, although I had to avert my eyes from Lady Katarina, feeling a little embarrassed by my grinning face.

I noticed that as I looked around, the other student council members were all smiling kindly at Lady Katarina too. Prince Jeord was his usual smiling self, and even the usually stoic Master Nicol had a faint smile about his lips.

I continued looking around the room... *Hmm? Something feels... off.* I moved my eyes to that person once more. As expected, he had his usual smile.

...Was I just seeing things? For a moment there, I thought he had the coldest expression on his face... It was gone as soon as I had shifted my gaze back to him — as if he had the same gentle expression about him all this time.

That was why I had assumed that it was just some sort of mistake on my part. After all... how could such a kind and gentle person ever have a look as cold as that... and to be glaring at Lady Katarina? It was all but impossible.

"Maria... these sweets are... delicious!" Lady Katarina said, a wide smile on her face, as I was lost in thought about what I had just seen.

I felt a wave of happiness wash over me once more, and soon enough, those thoughts were gone as quickly as they had appeared. *I should put even more effort into my baking, so that I can see this smile tomorrow, too!*

It had been ten years since my Light Magic had manifested. I had worked hard all this time, hoping that my wish would one day be granted. And now, after all this time... it finally had.

The first summer break since I had started at the academy arrived. While the summer breaks here were nowhere near as long as the ones in my previous life, I was happy that the Academy of Magic had any at all.

Most students returned home over the break, and I was no exception. I went back home to Claes Manor, where I was free once again to refine my anti-Catastrophic Bad End strategies.

Firstly, I teamed up with the head gardener, Grandpa Tom, to enhance the realism of my projectile snakes. This would be important if Jeord ever came at me with his blade.

I also read many books on agricultural methodology and theory, once again working the fields with a renewed passion — just in case I ever got exiled from the kingdom, and had to make a living as a farmer. However...

"Well, looks like I really do need to see the real thing..." I muttered, drawing the attention of my brother Keith, who had been next to me all this time.

"...Whatever are you up to this time, Big Sister...?"

"The fields, Keith! I want to see a real agricultural field!"

"...Fields? What do you mean by real? But there are fields right here!" Keith said, pointing to my many small fields that had slowly started invading the Claes Manor gardens with surprise written all over his face.

I had to set Keith straight about fields. "I mean *real* fields, Keith! Not these ones set up by hobbyists in some sort of garden! I want to see large, industrial-scale fields, run and owned by farming families!"

"...Why?"

"Obviously, because if certain events ever come to pass, this would ensure that I would be able to live as a capable farmer!" I said, puffing my chest out with pride.

Keith, however, simply held his head in his hands. "...I no longer know where or what to start commenting on..."

I continued extolling the virtues of having a look at real, industrial-scale fields of farming families to a seemingly exhausted Keith. Soon enough, he gave in and agreed.

A few days later, Keith and I sneaked out of the mansion, intending to go look at real agricultural fields... in disguise.

The reason we were in disguise was simple — if the daughter of a duke just showed up in the middle of some fields, the farmers who worked it would be shocked. And Mother would be angry if she found out. So we had to go incognito!

And so I dressed up as the daughter of a merchant family. Now that no one knew I was a noble, I was able to take an educational tour of the fields without causing a ruckus.

"As expected... the fields of a real farming family are really something else! The scale, structure, systems... all so very different!" I said after the tour had ended, staring out of the carriage we had borrowed from a merchant family.

It was fun to watch the scenery go by through the window. For a while, only large fields rolled by as the carriage moved along. But then the scenery started to change, and we were soon able to spot buildings in the distance.

"Ah! What is that, Keith?"

"Oh… that is a small town, Big Sister." Keith said, looking out of the same window I was.

"Wow, there's a town in a place like this!" I had been far too excited on the way to my educational tour, and as a result, hadn't noticed the town at all.

"Indeed. If memory serves, that happens to be Miss Maria Campbell's hometown."

"Oh?!"

What?! This place is Maria's hometown?! Actually, I heard she was born in a small town that was pretty far from the capital. But here, of all places? What a coincidence!

I see… so this is Maria's hometown… Hmm… now that I think about it…

"Then… wouldn't Maria be in that town right now? She did say that she would be going back home for summer break…"

"Hmm… Indeed, Big Sister. I do recall her saying something like… It can't be! You don't mean to—"

"Let's go visit, Keith!"

"…I knew it…"

Although Keith kept saying that we shouldn't bother them, I insisted that we could pop in for a quick visit. Eventually I managed to convince him, and so the two of us headed into the little town.

The town was a short distance away from the capital. It did indeed turn out to be small — just as I had heard from Maria. But although we had come all the way here in a great hurry, I realized that I had no idea where Maria lived.

Undeterred, I asked some of the townsfolk we passed by, and we were soon pointed in the direction of her house. I supposed this town was like the rural boonies that I had lived in in my previous life, where everyone knew each other's names and faces.

Once we had the info we needed, I charged all the way up to Maria's house with Keith.

"Hello… And who might you be…?" The woman who appeared in the doorway of the home was considerably beautiful — and resembled Maria strongly. I guessed that they must be related.

"Ah, um, I am Katarina Claes, a friend of Maria's. Would she happen to be available?" Although I had greeted the woman with a cheerful smile and upbeat tone, she seemed terribly surprised.

"…Maria is… momentarily out. I think she will return soon… If you would like, would you prefer to wait inside?"

With that, the woman invited Keith and me into her home. Although the Campbells lived in a normal house, one that most of the common citizens lived in, it was noticeably clean and tidy.

The woman introduced herself simply as Maria's mother. *Aha. Related by blood, as I thought.* The more I looked at her, the more I felt like she was much prettier, though also seemed to be more delicate, than my mother. At least she didn't seem like she would ever give her daughter a terrifying demon face.

Maria's mother invited us to take a seat at a table, which was probably their dining table, and then presented us with tea and sweets.

"Are these Maria's homemade sweets, too?" I asked.

Maria's mother, however, seemed even more surprised at this. "…No, I purchased them from a bakery in town. If I may ask… is she still baking sweets?"

"Yep! Maria is really good at it. I always ask if she can make them for me!"

"...You've been eating the sweets that... my girl makes?"

"Yes, all the time! They're always so delicious!"

For some reason, Maria's mother turned her gaze towards the ground at my words, before murmuring weakly, "I... see..."

Shortly after, the door opened and in came Maria, holding bags of groceries in her arms. She was shocked, at first, to see the two of us seated at her dining table.

"I thought I wouldn't be able to see you over this summer break, Lady Katarina... but I am so glad that we were able to meet," she said, looking happy at the sight of Keith and me.

After that, we spent hour after hour talking about one thing or another with Maria. Before I knew it, the sun had started to set, and we quickly made to leave the Campbell home.

Since we had come on this little adventure in disguise, we had borrowed the carriage from the merchant family we knew. But even a plain carriage would draw a lot of attention if it was left parked outside a commoner's house. So we'd had the coachman wait in the carriage at a plaza some distance away.

"I really should walk you to your carriage, Lady Katarina..." Maria said.

But I convinced her that she didn't have to go through the trouble. "This is just fine, Maria." It would be dinner time soon, after all, and Maria would surely be busy.

"Lady Katarina, Master Keith... Thank you very much for coming all the way here today."

"No, not at all! In fact, I should apologize for suddenly showing up at your door, Maria..."

"That's right. I do apologize as well, for our lack of consideration. I will ensure that word is sent ahead of time on our next visit."

After that short exchange, we turned and made to leave — and it was then that Maria's mother, who was silent with her head bowed for almost the entire time, approached us.

"…If I may… please. Please accept my gratitude for watching over my daughter," Maria's mother said, bowing to us deeply. The sight of Maria's beautiful mother, who Maria so closely resembled, bowing to us with such a serious expression was enough to make me a little nervous.

"Of course! We're happy to have her as a friend," I replied, bowing accordingly.

And with that, we turned once more, and hurried back to the carriage.

★★★★★★★★★

I was born in a small town, a short distance away from the capital. I was said to be the most beautiful girl in the town, and all the townsfolk were kind to me.

When I came of age, I was engaged to the most courageous, dependable, and popular man in the town. After we wed, I took on the Campbell name. We received the blessings of all the townsfolk, and had a wonderful wedding. A few years later, we had a daughter who looked just like me.

I named my beloved daughter "Maria." I had a wonderful husband and a sweet, beautiful daughter. My days were filled with happiness and joy.

That happiness, however, was all shattered the day magic manifested in my daughter.

"Magical aptitude" was a rare thing amongst the people of this kingdom. Furthermore, most of those who wielded magic were nobles. A commoner with such abilities was practically unheard of.

Due to the rarity of a commoner wielding magical powers, rumors spread that Maria was a child born out of an affair with a noble. Nothing but rumors, of course. I had never once betrayed my husband, and Maria was undoubtedly our daughter. However, talk of my supposed unfaithfulness spread like wildfire throughout the town.

My husband reassured me at first. "Don't worry. I don't suspect you of anything," he would say. However, the rumors became inflated over time, and perhaps it was all too much for him. Before I knew it, my husband stopped coming home altogether.

Even the townsfolk, whom we had gotten along with so well all this time, started distancing themselves from me. Before long, I had become fearful of their gazes, and started turning my eyes to the ground.

We were so blessed and happy before... How did it come to this? If only my daughter didn't have magic... If only I had never had such a child... I caught myself thinking such things, and it surprised me to realize that I had started resenting my daughter.

Maria had done nothing wrong. Even though I understood that logically, I couldn't quite control how I felt. As a result, I did all I could to avoid my daughter's gaze.

Even though I did next to nothing for my daughter, Maria excelled in spite of her circumstances. She was able to perfectly carry out her household chores and errands, and also scored high grades at the local school she attended.

Although everyone praised my daughter for being special, there were hidden barbs in their words. They meant that Maria was "special" because she was the love-child of myself and a noble, or that she had cheated at her tests with the aid of magic.

There were also many who offered to adopt Maria. *If I accept one of those offers... perhaps everything would work out.* I had such thoughts often, but in the end, I found myself unable to go through with it.

I was a terrible mother, continuing to avert my eyes from Maria. My daughter, however, merely kept smiling — as if her life depended on it. Even though she knew that I was a fool of a mother, Maria did not wish to let go of my hand.

To be honest, I had long since noticed that although Maria was praised as a genius, or as a special child, the truth of the matter was that she worked hard and was constantly striving to be better.

At the sight of that, I felt my resentment towards Maria slowly evaporating. However, I continued to avert my gaze from my daughter, because I feared what I would see if I looked at her once more.

Perhaps my daughter would no longer forgive me. Perhaps she could no longer overlook my transgressions. Perhaps her eyes would be filled with dislike... or even hatred.

Our eyes continued to avoid each other, and eventually my daughter came of age — she was fifteen, and left for the Academy of Magic. The house became quiet and incredibly lonely without her.

A few days ago, Mari returned home, apparently now on summer break. She now had a much brighter, cheerful expression on her face, especially when compared with how she was when she had left.

What exactly happened to my daughter across these few months? I would come face to face with the answer a few days later.

"Hello... And who might you be...?"

It was a little after noontime when I heard the knock. Upon opening the door, I found a young lady and young man, both about the same age as Maria. Although they were dressed in clothing that children of merchant families often wore, there was something different about them. They carried themselves with a regal aura.

"Ah, um, I am Katarina Claes, a friend of Maria's. Would she happen to be available?" the brown haired-girl said, as the boy next to her bowed politely.

Maria's... friends? I was shocked at these words. After all, Maria had been treated as an abnormality ever since her magic had manifested. As far as I knew, Maria had little in the way of friends.

"...Maria is... momentarily out. I think she will return soon... If you would like, would you prefer to wait inside?"

From the way she stood and the dignified air about her, I assumed that this girl and her companion would hardly want to enter a house like this. Maria's friends, however, didn't seem to mind.

Our house was small and cramped — we didn't even have a guest parlor. I had no choice but to seat them at the family dining table. The girl and her companion, however, didn't display the slightest hint of displeasure at this.

I quickly moved to prepare the best tea we had, in addition to laying out the best sweets the bakeries in this town had to offer. And then...

"Are these Maria's homemade sweets, too?" the girl suddenly asked.

I told her that they weren't, and then hesitantly asked if my daughter was still baking.

"Yep! Maria is really good at it. I always ask if she can make them for me!"

"...You've been eating the sweets that... my girl makes?"

"Yes, all the time! They're always so delicious!" the girl said with a smile.

A few years ago, Maria had brought the sweets that she practiced so hard to make to school. That evening, however, she returned with reddened eyes. Ever since, I had never seen her bring her homemade sweets to anyone.

My daughter, who would always force herself to smile in my presence, often cried alone, trying her best to not make a sound. I was a failure of a mother, who never did a thing for her.

Yet, in spite of all this, you've finally found friends... who will eat the sweets that you put so much love into...

After a while, Maria returned from her errands. Upon seeing the two seated at the table, she immediately broke into a bright smile. It was a smile that I had not seen for years — one of true happiness.

In these few months, my daughter had made such good friends, and was now able to be happy again. If my daughter changed... then I had to as well. I could not simply remain like this forever. If all I did was look at the ground and continue averting my eyes from Maria... perhaps one day I would be left behind. I had to change.

As the sun started to set, the girl and her companion turned to leave. It was then that I chased after them as quickly as I could.

"...If I may... please. Please accept my gratitude for watching over my daughter." I bowed deeply.

The girl merely smiled kindly. "Of course! We're happy to have her as a friend," she said, bowing in reciprocation.

Watching them walk into the distance, I finally turned, only for my gaze to meet with my daughter's. How many years had it been since I had looked at her like this? Her eyes were glistening with tears. And soon I found my vision distorting, too.

There was not a touch of hatred... or even dislike in her eyes. Instead, there was happiness reflected there. While we would not be able to return to how we were just overnight... perhaps, with time, we could both regain our lost days...

I approached Maria where she stood as the tears continued welling up in my eyes, before holding her shivering body in a tight embrace. Maria, who was just a little girl before, had already become as tall as I was.

★★★★★★★★★

After having unexpectedly met Maria and her beautiful mother, who looked uncannily similar to her daughter, I was in quite a good mood all the way until the carriage we had borrowed arrived at Claes Manor. I hummed a tune as I skipped straight through the front doors.

"Big Sister, if you go through the main doors with those clothes still on..." Keith seemed to be muttering something, but I couldn't hear him over my humming and skipping.

And then, as soon as I turned a corner in one of the hallways... I ran into none other than my villainess-faced mother, the origin of my own wicked looks. With her upwards-slanting, almond-shaped eyes, she stood in the hallway like some sort of indomitable sentry.

"…A-Ahh… Mother…"

"Welcome back, Katarina," Mother said, smiling. But her eyes weren't smiling at all. Almost immediately, an unsettling vibe filled the air. "Why, aren't you dressed in quite the strange attire?"

"Ah… Um. This is…" I panicked, only realizing now that I still had my merchant clothing on.

"Well, my questions on the clothing can wait. We can have a good discussion about it later… But Katarina, today while attending a tea party at a woman's association I frequent… I heard the strangest, strangest rumors. Rumors regarding the Academy of Magic, of course. Would you happen to know anything about that…?"

"…Strange… rumors?"

"But of course, Katarina. Very strange rumors, if I do say so myself. Of a certain individual who has set up a crop field in an isolated corner of the venerable Academy of Magic…"

"…"

"In addition, it would seem that this person is a student at the academy! I do wonder, though. Would such an individual exist, Katarina? A student, the child of a noble family… working in a field?"

"…"

"Isn't it the funniest thing you've ever heard, Katarina? But of course, no matter how I thought about it — about a noble child who would work in a field at the Academy of Magic, I mean — only a certain individual comes to mind. Perhaps we should have a talk in my room, Katarina."

With that, I was forcibly dragged into Mother's room, before being harshly lectured for three hours. From then on, I was forbidden from going outdoors during summer break, eating snacks, or working in the fields.

Lucky for me, Keith stepped in to help me out soon after. He managed to convince Mother that I was growing a field of flowers at the academy, and the reluctantly withdrew the punishments.

But still... what an eventful start to the summer.

It had been a few days since my visit to Maria's. I was relaxing at home, not really doing anything in particular (a great way to spend time, in my opinion), when I was suddenly invited by Jeord to go on a hike.

"It is quite hot, Katarina, is it not? Perhaps we should go for a dip in the cool waters of a nearby lake."

He was right; with the summer heat at its peak, going swimming in a lake sounded wonderful. It just so happened that Keith was away for some social gathering of young noble lords, and I was free either way. So I agreed to Jeord's proposal and started getting ready to go.

Under Jeord's recommendation, I ended up in the same carriage as him, and soon we were on our way to the lake. For some reason, it felt like Jeord had moved strangely close to me while we were in the carriage. Maybe I was just overthinking things. But just as I had arrived at this conclusion, the carriage came to a sudden stop.

Huh? What's this? A malfunction of some sort? I thought, surprised, only for the door of the carriage to slam loudly open. There, wheezing and breathless, was none other than Keith.

"Haa... Haa... Big Sister, are you alright?" Keith said, gasping for air between breaths. *What's that supposed to mean?*

"What are you talking about, Keith? I'm fine. There's nothing wrong, I was just going with Prince Jeord to the lake for a swim."

"...But... that is precisely where the danger is..."

"Hmm? More importantly, Keith. Weren't you away for that gathering of young noble lords today? Whatever are you doing here?"

Right, Keith had left early in the morning. Why would he suddenly show up halfway on the road to the lake? Now that I got a better look at him, I recognized the silhouette of the Claes carriage a short distance behind him. I hadn't asked Keith where exactly this gathering was held — maybe it was somewhere close to here? I asked him if that was the case.

"Well, not quite, Big Sister... in fact, it was held in a completely different location. I just so happened to run into Prince Alan before the gathering started. I heard from him that Prince Jeord had chosen to skip this gathering, and that he was here himself. That left me with a lingering feeling of dread... and I rushed back to the manor on gut instinct. As expected, Prince Jeord had left the grounds with you, Big Sister... All I could do was chase after you in a panic."

Oh, I see! So I guess that means... Keith really wanted to come have fun with Jeord and me. He must have been feeling left out! And here I was, thinking he was already all grown up. I suppose my brother still has a childish side to him. Eheheh.

"I understand, Keith. You were upset that you were excluded, right? Well then, let's go together."

"...Ugh, you really do not quite understand, do you Big Sister? In any case... I will be coming along too, Prince Jeord."

"...To think that I had specifically chosen this time, and even brought her all the way out here... I really am surprised at your dedication, Keith. But it is quite the pointless thing you have done, you fool of a brother..."

111

After that, there was a short discussion about whether I should switch to the Claes carriage. In the end, somehow, all three of us ended up in Jeord's carriage. Jeord and Keith sat next to each other, speaking enthusiastically with wide smiles on their faces. Meanwhile, I was left out of the conversation yet again, and decided to entertain myself by watching the passing scenery.

When we finally arrived at the lake, I was impressed by its grand beauty. Before I knew it, I was running this way and that, taking in the sights. But as expected, all that running soon tired me out, and I eventually wandered back to the carriage to fall asleep on the comfortable upholstery.

"Truly, she is ever so defenseless, is she not? Tell me, Keith. How exactly has the Claes family raised her?"

"To my knowledge, she was raised just as any noble lady should be…"

As I flitted in and out of my dreams, I thought I might have heard Jeord and Keith both let out loud, exasperated sighs.

A few days after our fun hiking trip, I found myself attending one of Prince Alan's performances with Mary. He would be playing the piano for this one.

The crowds that Alan's concerts drew were really amazing. In particular, the older noble ladies who came were always impressive. Although they quietly listened during the performance, the sheer volume of their cheers after he finished a piece reminded me of the idol concerts I'd attended in my previous life.

Amidst the thunderous applause, the performance ended — and soon, Mary had joined Alan, making the rounds as they accepted bouquets from the audience.

"Prince Alan, it was a wonderful performance, as always!"

"Yeah. Thanks." Alan's brusque response was in stark contrast to how he was during his performances. He always seemed so much more mature when he was performing, gleaming in the spotlight. I was sad that the performance was already over!

"You know, that last song today... I think it's the first time I've heard it. The crowd's cheers were really something else. Which song was that, Prince Alan?"

The applause after that one piece had been significantly louder than the rest. In fact, it sounded like some of the audience members had been literally wailing. The older noble lady who'd been sitting behind me had flushed cheeks, and was saying "Th-That song..." while fidgeting and whispering excitedly.

"It's the first time I've chosen to play that song, see. It's called... 'For You, My Beloved.'"

Ah, I see. It's a love song. Considering that Alan's repertoire didn't usually feature pieces like this, it made sense that the audience was riled up. But that meant...

"I see... 'For You, My Beloved'? So were you thinking of someone you liked as you were performing the piece?"

Perhaps it was his fiancée Mary — or maybe even the protagonist Maria. It was possible that even the childish Alan had become more of an adult. I threw in a faint smile as I asked about his potential crush.

"Eh? Someone I like? Wh-What's that supposed to mean...?"

"Hmm? But isn't it that sort of song, Prince Alan? The sort of song that you play while thinking of the person you love, I mean."

"M-Maybe that is the case... but i-it's not like I have anyone I like..."

Oooh. From that reaction, he definitely had someone in mind. Whether it was Mary or Maria, I thought that Alan beginning to walk the road to adulthood was a good thing for him.

"I-I... not really..." An intense blush had come over Alan's features as he seemed to be muttering something to himself.

"Prince Alan, the ladies are waiting for you. Perhaps it would be best if we greeted them posthaste," Mary said, sending Alan off to address the crowds while flashing a few glances in my direction. Her expression seemed a little forced, and I couldn't help but feel a little worried for her.

In the original setting of *Fortune Lover*, Mary had loved Alan greatly. But looking at her now, I didn't see any evidence of that. It didn't seem like she liked him in that way at all. Or maybe she was just put off by all the ladies in the audience fussing over him. Either way...

"...Um, Mary?" I thought I should say something to her in this situation.

"...Oh, that was most dangerous. He was a sliver away from becoming aware... To think that I've made so many preparations across the years to ensure that he would not notice... This calls for additional measures of obfuscation afterwards... I simply cannot have any more enemies surface at this stage..." Mary stood, muttering to herself with a serious expression on her face.

Aha, she does like Alan more than she lets on! In spite of the haphazard way she treats him... she must have another side to her love? Or maybe this is how she shows it? With that thought in mind, I silently prayed that the person Alan was thinking of while he played that love song was Mary, not Maria.

The day after the performance, I went out for a shopping trip with Sophia. Although my summer break wasn't quite as long as the ones in my previous life, I was making the most of the time I had. In fact, I completely forgot about the homework we were supposed to do during the break. Thoughts on that subject had long since sailed into the event horizon.

The plan for today was to visit various bookstores in town. Romance novels often started trending in towns like this one, so we might even find a few diamonds in the rough if we tried.

Sophia, in an effort to be less conspicuous, braided her hair and tucked it into her hat. Nicol, protective and loving as ever, came with us as an escort. But even without Sophia's hair showing, with Nicol's ravishing appearance, the siblings stood out whether they liked it or not. In fact, I could already feel the passionate gazes of both men and women around us... Amazing.

But since I lived my daily life surrounded by beautiful people, I soon forgot about the passionate gazes of the townsfolk. Instead, I was preoccupied with taking in the sights and sounds of the town, zipping around to all sorts of places. We were originally planning to only visit bookstores, but we ended up going to cute general stores, patisseries, and candy stores. I was taken in by their delicious-looking displays.

Sophia wasn't used to coming into town, but I dragged her all over the place throughout the day. Before I knew it, it was time for my friend to return home, and for me to return to Claes Manor.

"Haa! Today was so much fun!" I said, armed with bags of snacks and various trinkets in both my hands.

Sophia agreed earnestly. "Yes... It is the first time I've enjoyed myself... so much, while walking about in town..." she said, a healthy shade of crimson creeping into her face.

Given that I had dragged Sophia all over town today, I was worried that she wouldn't want to go on trips with me anymore. So her saying that made me feel relieved.

Soon enough, it was time for us to return by carriage.

"Ah! Lady Katarina... I enjoyed myself so much that I had forgotten... th-the most important thing I needed to do today!"

"Huh? What is it all of a sudden, Sophia?"

She seemed to have been overcome by a sudden realization.

"Ah, I, um... I f-forgot to purchase the one thing I... really wanted. I will quickly... go and fetch it."

Ah, she forgot to buy something. "In that case, I'll come too!" I offered.

"N-No. Some of my servants will come with me... I'll be fine! Please wait here with my brother, Lady Katarina... Um. Do your best, brother!" With a strangely suggestive smile, Sophia turned and rushed off in the general direction of the shops.

After that, I found myself alone with Nicol. "Ah, off she goes..." I murmured.

"It does appear so."

And that, as usual, ended my conversation with Nicol. But it would be a little awkward if we stayed quiet forever, so I decided to rack my brain for a topic of conversation. Before I could speak, however, Nicol broke the silence first — which was very rare.

"Thank you very much for today. It is the first time I have seen Sophia this happy on a trip to town."

"Oh, it was nothing. I had a lot of fun too!" Actually, I was sure I was the one who had the most fun on this trip. So much so that I wanted to tell him that I would love to do this again with them, but—

"Katarina Claes." For some reason, Nicol was now looking straight at me with burning flames of passion in his jet-black eyes. I felt my heart skip a beat — it was like my entire being was being trapped in his dark irises.

"My sister and I... are truly fortunate to have met you."

"Ah? Um, Master Nicol?" I stuttered, feeling myself slowly being sucked into his gaze. To make things worse, the sound of his voice was making me melt...! Frozen to the spot, I could only watch as Nicol lifted a single hand to my cheek.

"I know that an eternity is too much to ask. So... just for this moment. Please let me be by your side."

Nicol's almost-whispered words hit the circuitry of my mind with overwhelming force. I could feel my mind shorting out. I could no longer understand his words — I could only feel my head spinning from the sheer force of the Alluring Count's devilish charms.

Sometime during my mental short-circuit, Sophia returned. And so we boarded the carriage and set off on our journey home... But I had been done in by the devilish powers of the Alluring Count, and couldn't come up with a single topic of conversation with Nicol on the way back.

With this, I was once again overwhelmed by the fearsome power of the Count. From what Nicol had told me during my birthday party last year, I had deduced that Nicol's love interest was a married woman, or maybe a man. Given his terrifying powers, I felt like there was no one alive who could withstand his advances...

All I could do was pray that Nicol would not go astray as he walked his path of forbidden love.

Over summer break, I found myself at a ball organized by some noble house, and it was there that I ran into the student council president. The president was very popular at the academy, so naturally, he was popular at the ball too.

In particular, he was approached a lot by noble ladies around his age. Apparently, he hadn't formally announced a marriage engagement yet. That was rare, considering he was the oldest son of a marquess, and that he was seventeen years old.

Of course, the Claes family had someone like that too — my brother, who still hadn't issued a formal engagement declaration. The president, like Keith, was constantly approached by so many potential partners that he could afford to deflect any of them easily.

Or maybe the members of his fanclub were similar to the fans of the Alluring Count, who, through surveillance and interference, placed immense pressure on anyone who dared approach Nicol. Of course, they would all have to give up eventually...

Curious, I greeted the president and decided to find out why he had refused all those noble ladies. "Perhaps you aren't very interested in becoming engaged, President?"

Upon hearing my question, a troubled expression came over his lovable face. "Ah, it is not quite like that... You see, everyone is so wonderful. It is very difficult to decide."

Oh! So the president's case is less like Nicol's, and more like Keith's... unable to decide, they just keep refusing everyone who asks. In that case...

"Perhaps there's someone that you already have in mind...?"

After all, it seemed like Keith had someone he liked. I'd had that feeling for a long time now. Although I had originally assumed that he was interested in Maria, I realized that this couldn't be right, since he'd seemed that way even before meeting her. Was it someone else, then...? Though now he seemed to be obsessed over Maria after all. Hmm? I didn't really get it.

Was the President rejecting all potential partners because he already had someone in mind? Curious, I asked once again.

"Someone I have... in mind?" For a moment, the president's expression turned harsh. In that moment, he seemed very different from his usual self. I started to panic, thinking I had upset him with my rude questions.

"Ah, um, I..."

"No one."

"...Eh...?"

"It is as I said. I have no one in mind," the president said, as his sharp gaze — as sharp as his words, locked onto me. I felt an involuntary shiver go down my spine.

"U-Um... President...?"

The president was acting shockingly different from his usual, calm self. I stood there tensely, unsure how to respond.

"Yes. The dance begins soon, Lady Katarina. Your partner, Prince Jeord, is already waiting for you in that corner over there," the president said, once again with his usual smile and calm demeanor.

What? Did I imagine all that? But even though I still felt confused, I ended up getting lost in a passionate conversation about romance novels with Sophia and Mary, and I forgot all about the strange incident.

My short but fulfilling summer vacation eventually came to a rapid end. But...

"Keith, please! I still haven't finished this... and this... and that!"

"...Big Sister. What exactly have you been doing for the entirety of this break...? You have not done any of your homework? How many times have I reminded you? How many times have you said 'I promise I'll do it'? And in the end you have not even touched a single... question. Whatever will you do? We are already slated to return to the academy tomorrow..."

"B-But! I've done a little bit...!"

"And by 'a little bit'... would you happen to mean these few words, written in this one book?"

"...I'm sorry, Keith..."

"In any case... I suppose I do have to take responsibility for taking your words at face value, Big Sister..."

My words at what value now...? Ugh... how could you, brother...!

"We have no other choice. We will have to ensure that it is done before we return to the academy. I will help."

"...Alright..."

That was why I ended up staying up all night just two days before we returned to the academy, doing my best to complete my assignments. I felt like my head was swirling as my thoughts were shrouded by a severe lack of sleep.

Come to think of it, this was how I finished my summertime assignments in my previous life, too. Ah... how nostalgic.

"So how is it? *Fortune Lover*, I mean. Have you played much?" my otaku friend, Acchan, asked with a slight grin over lunch break.

"I've done the arrogant prince and the playboy, but I just can't get to that terrible sadistic prince... The rival character, that villainous noble lady, interferes too much!"

Acchan's grin seemed to only widen as I sighed, complaining about my lack of progress. "Heh heh. I've already cleared all the routes!"

"Wha?! All of them?! Already?"

"Yep! The four potential love interests were a given, but I've also cleared the hidden character's route! It's all done!" Acchan said, an invincible smile on her face. Once again, I found myself gazing at my otaku friend with awe and respect.

"Ah... of course you did, Acchan... You're so fast! Wait... so there was a hidden character, like we thought?"

"Yes. If you clear the routes of the four main characters, that hidden one opens up. So... do you want to know who it is? Do you?"

"W-Wait! Don't tell me... no spoilers!" I said, covering my ears.

Acchan smiled mischievously, leaning in slowly. "The hidden character is..."

"Nooo! Lalala! I'm not listening!!"

"Young miss, it is already morning. Please wake up."

"N-No… I don't wanna… I don't wanna hear it…!"

"Young miss. Please do stop lazing around. If you do not wake up soon, you will miss your morning lessons."

"…Hnn…?"

The first thing I saw when I opened my eyes was my personal maid, Anne. Specifically, it was Anne standing with her hands on her hips, looming over me.

"Oh… Anne. Good morning."

"Yes. A very good morning to you too, young miss. If you are indeed awake, then please do make the adequate preparations."

As I stared at Anne, who was weaving through the room and preparing one thing or another, I started to remember something about the dream I'd just had. The cogs in my mind had barely started moving.

"I feel like I… just had a really… important dream…"

"…A dream, young miss?" Anne responded, noticing me murmuring to myself.

"Yes… a dream that I was having… until just now. For some reason, I feel like it was a really important dream… But of course, I always forget dreams immediately after I wake up…"

"…Is that so? I did hear you talking in your sleep, but it really did not sound like anything of much importance."

"Hmm? Really?" *Then maybe it was just… my imagination?* Nope. I couldn't remember what kind of dream it was at all. Though if Anne said it wasn't important, then it probably wasn't.

Was I just imagining that it was important? Am I just overthinking things…? Well, there was nothing I could do about it now. I forgot about it and started my morning routine.

Before I knew it, half a year had passed since I had started at the Academy of Magic. The seasons started to change, too — the colors of autumn soon gave way to the frosty winds of winter.

I was now good friends with Maria, the protagonist of *Fortune Lover*. And I had gotten closer with some of my classmates outside of the student council, too. All in all, I was settled into my life at the academy.

Of course, I was constantly fighting my drowsiness, and my magic hadn't improved at all. In other words, everything was normal. No matter how many tests I had to take, all I had to do was look at my friends' notes, study what I could, and then I'd skate by with average grades.

Nicol and the student council president, in particular, were great at tutoring me on various subjects, and I was very much indebted to the both of them. I really had wonderful friends.

The fields were doing well, and I had slowly perfected my snake-tossing motions. From my perspective, I was fully prepared for any kind of incoming Catastrophic Bad End.

There was, however, one thing I still couldn't figure out — the all-important information on who exactly Maria's love interest was. It was the same for all the other potential love interests. I had no idea who they liked, which was bad, considering that this information would heavily influence future events.

No matter how much I asked Maria who she liked, she would always derail the conversation by responding with, "I really respect *you*, Lady Katarina."

Maria had no idea that she was incredibly popular. "The boys in the student council are all dazzled by your charm, Maria!" I would say.

"That is all but impossible, Lady Katarina. After all, there is already someone else that everyone has been charmed by," Maria would say with a surprised expression.

How could that be possible? The charismatic love interests of Fortune Lover *leaving behind the charming Maria, and instead looking at someone else...? There's no such person.*

While I did think that Maria was doing her best, as usual, I supposed this was just her protagonist traits kicking in. Specifically, her amazing capacity to be "dense," and have creative "misunderstandings."

Even Keith, who had assisted me when I investigated Maria a while ago, muttered, "Really... how dense could you be?" Judging from his words, I guessed that even Keith thought that Maria's denseness was on another level. Even the potential love interest characters would have a hard time keeping up with this level of... density.

And so, I continued living my peaceful life at the academy, with everything going well, other than that one question about who Maria and the others liked. Perhaps that was why it felt so sudden.

Finally... the gears were set in motion. The game was afoot.

On the lunch break of a particularly chilly day, I headed towards the dining hall with a few of my classmates. Usually, my friends, brother, or other members of the student council would be with me. But today they all seemed somewhat busy, and told me that they would join me another time.

When I look back on it, that was what was different about that day. All of my friends were busy at the exact same time; they all needed to finish some extra work, so they had to miss the lunch break. This had happened before, but never to all of them at once.

At the time, I didn't question this turn of events. My mind was filled with thoughts of what that afternoon's lunch menu would be. That was when it happened — while I was strolling, unawares, into the dining hall.

"Katarina Claes. We have some important things to talk about." Standing before me as I took my first step into the dining hall was a noble lady who had very high social standing.

Specifically, she had been the one who was widely expected to become Jeord's fiancée — at least, until I came into the picture. While she often hissed insults at me under her breath and spent a good deal of her time staring at me, I had never seen her speak to me upfront and in person.

With her similarly upward-slanting eyes and thin lips, she shared similar villainess features with me. At one point, I had even thought of her as a villainess-faced comrade.

The mean-faced student narrowed her eyes, accentuating her unfriendly appearance. Completely baffled, I stood rooted to the spot, staring at her. It was then that I noticed the dozen or so other students behind her. Much like their ringleader, those girls were staring at me too. As expected, the students behind her were the very same ones who always gossiped behind my back.

The scene felt somehow… familiar.

"Katarina Claes. We will expose your numerous wrongdoings today, here and now!" the noble lady before me said, her voice echoing loudly off the dining hall's walls.

Under normal circumstances, the dining hall would be a hive of activity — natural, given that half of the academy's students were usually gathered here at this time. But now the room was silent, and I could suddenly feel the gazes of all its patrons focusing on me.

As if pleased by this development, the girl's lips curled upwards. All I could do was stand and stare, too stunned to even speak a word, having suddenly been thrust into the center of attention.

My "numerous wrongdoings"...? But what could those be? Tossing projectile snakes? But it's not like I've thrown those at other people. I don't feel like I've done anything to cause trouble...

Or is it because I tilled a field on the academy grounds? That I carried out agricultural activities in such a prestigious place...? Something like that?

The noble lady before me, however, didn't seem to notice or care that I was lost in my own thoughts. Instead, she continued.

"You, the daughter of a duke and Prince Jeord's fiancée, have been observed abusing your power and social standing on multiple occasions, using these privileges to oppress those who have no choice but to bend to your will! Not only that, you have also been bullying Maria Campbell, Wielder of Light, and favored member of the student council! Time and time again, you have subjected Maria to horrible bullying and intimidation!"

"Huh?!"

Her words reminded me of a particular scene — and it was then that I remembered that I had seen all this somewhere before.

This was the one event I had witnessed countless times when playing through *Fortune Lover*: the Public Prosecution of Katarina Claes. Here, the many sins and wrongdoings of Katarina the Villainess would be exposed, and she would face the collective judgment of the student body.

I couldn't believe I had been on alert this whole time, earnestly avoiding various Bad Ends, only to end up in the middle of this terrible situation. I gazed blankly at the noble lady standing before me, still in a daze. Everyone was staring at me with faces full of tension.

But… something about all this was… off. While this event was unmistakably "the Public Prosecution of Katarina Claes," the ones who normally confronted her with these sins were the members of the student council — in other words, all the potential love interest characters of *Fortune Lover*.

In Jeord's route, he would be standing in front of Maria, as if to shield her. In Keith's, he'd be the one doing that instead. But either way, I saw no sign of them now.

I was confused. Why were these noble ladies standing where the student council should have been, and why were they accusing me of doing things like that?

"Playing dumb won't save you! I have proof of your wrongdoings right here, in my hands! We even have a witness!"

Saying so, the girl raised a sheaf of papers to my face, before tilting her head slightly, gesturing to her one of her subordinates, who was still glaring at me.

Written on the paper were countless examples of bullying and hurtful behavior directed towards Maria. I had no memory of any of these events, of course, but I was made out to be the culprit of the acts on these papers. In addition, the so-called witness testified that she saw me hurt Maria on multiple occasions.

As the accusations were slung at me rapidly, I, as well as all the students in the dining hall, could only listen on, stunned. Soon, an uneasy blanket of silence covered the dining hall. The students of the academy seemed to collectively hold their breaths, as if they were watching for some sort of reaction.

It was then that they arrived — Maria and my childhood friends, the members of the student council. They appeared from the other side of the dining hall, behind the group of noble ladies who were accusing me, and soon approached us.

"What, exactly, is transpiring here?" Jeord said, amidst the painfully still and tense atmosphere. He eyed the noble ladies and me with a questioning gaze.

In response, the noble lady who was once the most promising candidate for the position of Jeord's fiancée began explaining my various supposed misdeeds, just as she had done before.

The student council members before me — my childhood friends, my adopted brother, and even Maria's expressions began to slowly twist. *Ah, this was exactly what happened during the Public Prosecution of Katarina Claes... But normally, only Jeord or Keith would be here...*

Maria's current expression was just like how it was in *Fortune Lover* as she stood behind Jeord or Keith. In the original setting, she would muster up her courage — and with unwavering eyes, step out from behind Jeord or Keith, confronting the villainous Katarina, whose evil acts had been finally exposed. And then say...

"This is the truth, and nothing but the truth! I have always been bullied and hurt by Lady Katarina Claes!"

The students in the dining hall, in turn, would be in awe at Maria's dignified attitude, silent strength, and courageous stance.

As I was reminiscing about *Fortune Lover*'s scenario, the noble lady had finally finished rattling off her lengthy list of accusations. And then, just like in the game, Maria stepped out from the shadows to stand at the front of the crowd.

Having awakened the memories of my past life, I wasn't at all like the original Katarina Claes. Unlike her, I hadn't done anything wrong. And yet, things were progressing just like they did in the game. At this rate, I'd soon come face to face with a Catastrophic Bad End. I would either be exiled from the kingdom, or killed by Maria's love interest.

Do I have a snake in my pocket right now...? If I were exiled from the kingdom, would I be able to at least take my favorite farming hoe with me...?

Maria's eyes were filled with an aura of unwavering will, just like how I remembered them. And then, slowly, she spoke.

"These are lies! These accusations are nothing but lies and slander! I have never once been subject to any of these things by Lady Katarina Claes!" Her dignified voice echoed throughout the silent dining hall.

And then, Maria turned to face the noble ladies, as if to shield me from harm. "How could you come up with such false accusations? How *dare* you insult someone I hold so dear?!" Her voice was like nothing I had ever heard before — it was a steely, determined voice.

Although the noble ladies initially froze up at Maria's shocking reaction, they soon resumed their assault. "Whatever are you talking about, Maria Campbell! We are doing this for you! We are exposing Katarina Claes' wrongdoings out of consideration for you!"

"That's right! These aren't lies or slander! We have written testimony, evidence, and even a witness! You are the one who is being deceived by that evil woman!"

"Exactly! To be tricked by such a detestable woman... how pitiful, how sad! Maria Campbell... *we* are your allies."

The noble ladies kept going, each bolder than the last.

"But alas... to claim circumstantial evidence such as this as real evidence? Most amusing, is it not...?" Jeord said, holding the sheaf of papers in one hand.

Although Jeord had suggested that the situation was amusing, there was not a single trace of a smile on his face. Instead, his expression was stoic, almost chilling. If the usually impassive Nicol was the one who had delivered this line, it would have been one

129

thing. But this was Jeord we were talking about... the prince who always had a smile on his face.

Jeord's blank expression, as well as the slowly expanding aura of pressure that he was exerting, soon caused the noisy noble ladies to clam up completely. Up until a moment ago, they were so eagerly chattering on. Now, however, they pursed their lips and stared at him fearfully.

"In any case... it would be all but impossible for my simple-minded and pure sister to carry out such specific and detailed acts of bullying. If I may say so... I usually spend my time by my sister's side. However, I do not recall seeing this witness of yours... not once. Did you genuinely see my Big Sister, Katarina Claes, carry out these specific acts...?" Keith said, looking up from the paper of detailed accusations.

On his face was a cold smile — one that I had never seen before. A single glance from Keith was enough to cause the so-called witness to retreat, giving an involuntary squeak as she took a few steps backwards.

"Honestly! Lady Katarina would never do such a thing! It is as Master Keith says — Lady Katarina is simple and pure! She is incapable of such intricate and complicated plans!" Mary declared with a tense expression.

Immediately after, Alan spoke up too, in his usual brusque manner. "That's right! There's no damn way this idiot could plan something difficult like that! She's stupid, see?! All she can do is face you in a sincere one-to-one!"

Sophia chimed in next. "Exactly so…! Lady Katarina would never do anything like this… planning behind someone's back?! She is not capable of it! Lady Katarina simply does not have the capacity to act in such a way!!"

"Well said," added Nicol.

Although everyone seemed to be protecting me from these outlandish accusations… for some reason, I couldn't help but feel like they were severely underestimating my capabilities…

And then, as soon as my friends delivered their statements, the familiar voices of a few classmates started ringing out through the dining hall.

"Yes! Lady Katarina would never do anything of the sort!"

"Lady Katarina bullying another student? Unthinkable!"

The voices rose up, one after the next. Soon they grew louder, flooding in from all corners of the room. And then…

"It is as everyone says," Maria said firmly. "Lady Katarina is not the kind of person to bully or hurt another! While the accusations and details written on this paper about me being bullied are true… Lady Katarina was in no way the perpetrator! In fact, Lady Katarina herself protected me from these bullies, time and time again! Also… I clearly remember the faces of those who really did bully me and attempt to cause me harm. If there is really a need, perhaps I should name them, one by one, here and now…"

It was as if she were someone else. The usually gentle, calm, and soothing Maria… was now courageously deflecting the accusations directed at me, swatting them away one by one. From the corner of my eye, I could see a few people seated in the dining hall slowly turning pale. And some of the noble ladies who were accusing me reacted the same way, lowering their heads.

The attackers were now obviously at a disadvantage. No longer able to continue their accusations, their voices slowly grew softer and softer, sharply contrasting their initial tone. Soon, they trailed out of the dining hall.

Immediately, Maria came to my side to reassure me, as I had been silent during the entire ordeal. "Lady Katarina, are you alright?" she asked, looking straight into my eyes with an expression of pronounced worry.

I nodded deeply. "Yeah... I'm fine. Um... Thank you, everyone," I said to my friends, as well as the other students who had spoken up for me.

"No... In fact, I apologize, Katarina. For not being at your side when this began," Jeord said, placing a hand on my shoulder.

"Sorry we were late, Big Sister," Keith added, doing the same.

Before I knew it, the tension in my shoulders had faded away. And with that came a deep, familiar rumbling. It would seem that my stomach, still empty, was at its limit.

"I never thought those girls would dare to do something like this to Katarina."

"I agree, Prince Jeord. While it is indeed true that they view Big Sister as an enemy of sorts... I did not think that they would go this far."

"Yeah. Even if she was doing all that stuff, she's still the daughter of a duke. It's stupidly dangerous for them to do something like that. I can't believe it."

"Also, there is the matter of this evidence... no matter how one would spin it, I hardly believe that their little group is capable of such. The level of fabrication is simply too high."

"It is as Lady Mary says… I do not think that those students are… capable of creating such well-crafted pieces of fake evidence…"

"…It is also odd that we were all summoned at the same time to perform various tasks."

While I was finally able to tuck into my much-deserved lunch, my friends all seemed to be talking about something complicated. But I was just happy that I'd survived the Public Prosecution of Katarina Claes and avoided a Catastrophic Bad End.

Given that the scenario of *Fortune Lover* officially ends during the graduation ceremony next spring, I still couldn't let down my guard… But even so, I had gotten out of that terrible situation thanks to everyone's help. That was enough reason to celebrate.

I was caught up in my own thoughts, and didn't notice that Maria alone was silent, as if thinking about something important. With lunch break finally over, everyone was just about to return to afternoon classes… when Maria suddenly spoke up.

"There is someplace I would like to go. Please go on ahead, everyone."

"Should I go with you, Maria?" Although it seemed like the bullies were finally going to leave her alone, I was still worried about her.

"No… it is nothing important. I will be fine on my own. Please, do go on ahead," Maria said, staunchly refusing my offer.

Maybe her stomach hurts? Does she need to use the washroom? Maybe she shouldn't have eaten so much over lunch break…

"Hmm. Alright then. Afternoon lessons start soon though, so make sure to come back quickly."

"Of course, Lady Katarina," Maria replied with her usual smile, before heading off in the opposite direction of the classrooms.

After this, I would deeply regret not having gone with Maria.

Even though I told her to come back quickly, she didn't show up to class. Thinking that she was sick, I checked the infirmary, but she wasn't there either.

After this, we all searched for Maria… but no matter how hard we tried, we couldn't find her anywhere. It was as if Maria Campbell had vanished into thin air after we had parted ways at the end of the lunch break.

It was now the second day since Maria's sudden disappearance. Although my friends and I desperately searched the academy for her, we could find no trace of her at all — not a single clue.

All I could do was panic, my mind a hysterical mess. *Why didn't I just go with her…?* As the days went by, I regretted that decision more and more.

"Here. Drink this and warm up. You look terrible, Lady Katarina," said the student council president as he handed me a cup of freshly brewed tea.

"…Thank you very much," I said, gratefully accepting the cup. It had the same gentle taste, and its warmth soon spread through my body.

I was in the council chambers, as I always was. I stared at the chair that Maria used to sit in. Normally, after the president would offer me tea, Maria would bring me some of her homemade treats, all smiles. But now that smile was gone.

"Miss Campbell has a good head on her shoulders, and wields strong Light Magic. I am sure she will be alright," the president said, attempting to soothe me as my gaze remained fixed on the empty chair — Maria's chair. The president had assisted us in searching for her, and even attempted to cheer me up in his always-gentle voice. Even now, he was showing me so much consideration.

I knew I wasn't the only one suffering; I could tell that my friends felt the same way. After all, the president was close with Maria too. He would definitely feel her absence as much as we did. Even so, he had taken the time to cheer me up. *Wallowing in regrets and being depressed won't help anything. I should put those feelings aside and do what I can.*

I'll definitely find you. Please be okay. Wait for me... Maria.

It was the night of the third day that Maria had gone missing. After eating dinner at the dormitory, I was heading back to my room to prepare for the next day. It was then that Jeord invited me to his quarters with a grave expression on his face.

It was pretty late for social calls — but beyond that, Jeord's severe expression made my stomach drop.

"What is it..? Don't tell me... Has there been news of Maria...?" I asked, my voice quivering.

Jeord simply shook his head. "Not quite. We still have not located Maria. However... we have discovered something that might be related to her disappearance. I thought to inform you posthaste."

"Something related to her disappearance?"

"First... look at this." Jeord presented me with a sheaf of papers. They were the very same papers that had listed all my supposed sins and wrongdoings, the ones that were shoved in my face earlier that week.

"This is... from before..."

"Indeed, the documents those nobles confronted you with the other day. Something about these papers caught my attention, and I've been investigating them alongside Maria's disappearance..."

Jeord had long been aware of those noble ladies that had attempted to frame me at the Public Prosecution of Katarina Claes.

He knew that they hated me, but since they didn't have the social standing or power to cause me any real harm, he had decided to leave them be.

Yet in spite of Jeord's assessment, they had managed to hurt me. The problem was that those noble ladies shouldn't have had the resources to create the accusatory documents they'd used against me. Jeord couldn't overlook this glaring contradiction, and he had been looking into it as well as searching for Maria. And then...

"Most peculiar, is it not? The conclusion is obvious — those nobles were not the ones who created these documents."

"...What does that mean, then?"

"Another party was responsible for this. Indeed, when questioned, the nobles claim to have no memory of how they came across these papers in the first place."

"But how could they not remember? That makes no sense..."

"Of course, it was most unbelievable. Even I thought that they were lying at first, and conducted my own investigation... but it would seem that they were all telling the truth."

"..."

They didn't even know where their so-called evidence came from? They got it from someone else? No way. They waved it around with such confidence!

Then again, using those papers as evidence is ridiculous. Did they all lose their memories about the whole thing...?

Still wearing that same severe expression, Jeord continued on despite my stunned silence. "Alas, it goes even deeper. For some reason, all of those involved seem to have absolutely no memory of the events that transpired... for that entire day."

"...Wha?!"

"It is beyond a doubt that those girls harbor ill will towards you... that much is plain. However, it is unthinkable that they would be so bold as to publicly level accusations against you."

Jeord had a point — those noble ladies did dislike me. In fact, they would often curse me under their breaths if I walked past them by myself. Even so, they didn't seem to have the guts to actually try to harm me.

After all, I was the daughter of a duke, and the fiancée of the third prince of the kingdom. I had plenty of political power, so any attempt to attack me without sufficient backup would just backfire with terrible consequences. While the ladies involved had higher social standing than the average noble, I couldn't see any of them having the nerve to pick a fight with Katarina Claes herself, especially in public.

Even so... these events did happen. For some reason, those girls were all overcome with an irresistible urge to conduct a great counterattack against the "terrible oppressor" Katarina Claes... And that feeling appeared in not one, but all of them at the same time.

Once they left the dining hall, those emotions apparently faded and the girls were left clutching their heads, wondering why they did such a thing. When Jeord interrogated them about it, they were all apologetic for their actions.

"But... if what you say is true, then that's really suspicious. In fact... it almost seems like those nobles were being controlled by someone else... against their will."

Jeord's expression immediately darkened. "If I had to say, Katarina... it would not be an assumption, but a definite reality. Those nobles were being controlled by someone."

"Huh...?!"

"The overall demeanor of those girls was indeed strange at the time..."

"B-But... controlled? By someone else? Is that..."

Controlling something like an earthen golem is one thing, but actual, living humans...?

Anyway, I've never heard of anything like hypnotism in this world. Is it even possible to control the minds of that many people at once...? I was truly confused.

Jeord continued his explanation once more, looking more and more grave with each passing moment. "To control the mind of another, yes... it is indeed possible — with the power of Dark Magic, that is."

"...What? Dark... Dark Magic? Is there even such a thing?"

From what I understood, the magical elements in this world were Water, Fire, Earth, Wind, and Light. Those born with magical ability would have their powers manifest at a certain age. This was what I had been taught by the academy, and even the tutors who educated me in my childhood. Everyone knew this much.

There were only five kinds of magic — Water, Fire, Earth, Wind, and Light. No one told me about any other kinds of magic, not even here at this prestigious academy.

"Yes, Katarina. The sixth magic... Dark Magic. Those who wield magic woven from such magical energies, the Dark Arts, are capable of controlling the hearts of others. 'Wielders of Darkness,' so to speak."

"...But I haven't... Dark Magic? Dark Arts? I've never heard of anything like that..."

"Of course. Dark Magic is a very dangerous thing. It is forbidden, and often hidden away. Only certain individuals in this kingdom know of its concept and existence."

"Dangerous...?"

"It is the ability to control the hearts of others. Those who fall prey to this domination have absolutely no memory of it. A most fearsome magic, is it not?"

To have your own mind controlled without warning... and have no memory of what you could have done during that time. He was right, that was a terrifying idea.

"As such, it is fair to conclude that the ladies involved in this particular incident were being controlled by someone who wields Dark Magic. In other words, Katarina... this incident may very well be the result of you being targeted by a Wielder of Darkness."

"...Me? Targeted? By a Wielder of Darkness? ...Why?" While most of the noble ladies just disliked me because of the fact that I was Jeord's fiancée... had I done something else to make them angry?

"I know not of the reasons, Katarina. We do not even have any suspects lined up. However... it would do you well to be cautious. Take care to avoid solitary movements from now on, if you would..."

"...I understand..."

I thought that the problem of the girls harassing me had already been solved with everyone's help... But it turns out that there was something much more ominous going on here.

But wait... why would a Wielder of Darkness be targeting me? And if I was their target, then why...?

"Why did Maria disappear, then...?" If I was the one the Wielder of Darkness wanted, then Maria shouldn't have been involved.

"Ah, well… Assuming that this mystery individual's target was you, Katarina, Maria should have been left alone. However… Maria Campbell is a Wielder of Light."

"Yes, that's true… but what does that have to do with anything?"

"It is said that those born with Light Magic are able to sense Dark Magic when it is used. They are opposites, you see. It is even said that only those with Light Magic are capable of identifying the Dark Arts when they are used."

"What?! Then, Maria was…"

"She most likely picked up on something during the incident and made contact with this Wielder of Darkness. It is my assumption at this point that she has been kidnapped by this individual."

The Dark Arts… Magic that was capable of dominating the mind of another. Had Maria sensed it? More importantly, where had she been taken to? I felt my head spinning at all the information I was taking in. I couldn't make sense of any of it.

I didn't even know Dark Magic existed before now. A forbidden magic that was hidden away… *Oh? But then, what happens to people who are born with it?*

"…But… if Dark Magic is dangerous and kept a secret, what happens to people who are born with it? Do they hide their powers? And anyway, how can they possibly keep tabs on these Wielders of Darkness once their powers awaken?" I asked, immediately wanting to know more.

"You see, unlike other kinds of magic, Dark Magic is not something that one is simply born with. The Dark Arts, are a new type of magical power, obtained sometime later in a magically capable individual's life."

"Obtained later in life...? A new type of magical power...?" *Aren't magical powers determined at birth? How could someone get magic later on in life?*

As if sensing my growing confusion, Jeord continued his explanation with a lowered voice. "To obtain Dark Magic, a certain ritual is required."

"A ritual?"

"Yes. It is said that... if a certain something is offered up as a sacrifice in that ritual, the one performing it would become a Wielder of Darkness."

"A sacrifice?"

Jeord nodded deeply at my question, frowning, before taking in a deep breath and going on. "You see... according to what we know about this ritual, one becomes a Wielder of Darkness... when a human life is offered up as a sacrifice. As such, anyone who wields Dark Magic would have obtained it through an exchange. It is magic traded for the life of another."

I was in a sea of darkness. Pitch black. I stood in a world where I could not tell up from down.

At my feet were the fallen bodies of all of my dear friends. Jeord, Keith, Mary, Alan, Sophia, Nicol, and Maria. There was no hint of life in their faces.

"Everyone... wake up! Please wake up!" I shouted as if my life depended on it. I shook each and every one of them desperately. They didn't move at all.

"...Why...? How... did this happen?" I knelt down amongst the unmoving bodies of my friends. I could feel myself shivering, the tears welling up in my eyes.

How could this happen...? How could I lose everyone I care for...? If this is the end we are coming to... then it should have been just me. Just me who faced disaster...

"Why...? Why...?"

My tears continued to flow silently in this pitch-black world.

When I opened my eyes, I was greeted with the familiar ceiling of the dorm room I had been living in for the past six months. The room was dark. I couldn't see any light outside my window, so I figured that the sun hadn't risen yet.

"Was that... a dream?" My voice was quivering and faint. I could feel my body shaking.

I was covered in cold sweat. I placed a few fingers on my cheek, and found that they were wet. Apparently I was crying as I lay in bed, dreaming.

What a terrible nightmare... I held myself as tightly as I could.

To become a Wielder of Darkness, one had to exchange another's life. Maybe it was because of that terrible fact that I'd had such a horrible dream.

But that future was impossible. There was no way it would happen. In the original game, the only person at risk of dying was the rival villainess character, Katarina Claes. And that only happened in Alan, Keith, and Jeord's routes.

To be fair, I hadn't cleared Nicol's route yet. But then again, the rival in that scenario was Sophia. Nicol, who loved his sister dearly, would never do anything bad to her. So there was no way anything like that could happen.

I, Katarina Claes, was the only one who was in danger in this game world. I'd spent the last seven years of my life preparing to overcome that danger.

"It'll be okay," I said to myself. But no matter how hard I tried to forget, the vision I had seen in that nightmare wouldn't fade.

In the end, I never fell back asleep.

The next morning, I started feeling sick. Probably because I hardly got any sleep the night before after seeing such a gruesome sight in my dreams. Keith and Jeord came with me to the infirmary, where I could hopefully get some rest.

Maybe it was because I hadn't slept enough, or because I was reassured at seeing their faces, but I fell asleep almost immediately after I was tucked into the warm bed.

When I woke up, quite some time had passed. It was now almost lunch break, and Jeord and Keith had returned to their classes. My head was clear now after the short nap, so after thanking the nurse, I started heading back to class.

Although Jeord had warned me not to go anywhere alone just the day before, it was only a short walk between the infirmary and the classroom, so I figured it would be okay. The quickest route would be to cut across the courtyard, and that was the route I took.

Warm sunlight shone down on me as I stepped outside. It didn't take long for my eyes to settle on a small bench — the very same one where Maria planned to eat her lunch, not too long ago.

Maybe I can dawdle a little longer. What harm could it do? I approached the bench and sat down on it slowly. Before I had gotten to know Maria, she would always eat here by herself.

Maria is sweet and gentle... I thought that we could be friends forever. I wonder where she is now...?

If what Jeord said yesterday was true, then Maria was in a lot of danger... After all, it was possible that she had been taken away by a Wielder of Darkness — someone who had already sacrificed the life of another to gain their powers.

"Lady Katarina? Whatever are you doing here?"

I turned around at the sudden voice that called my name. Standing there was the president, smiling at me with his usual charming smile.

"Ah… I was feeling a little sick, and so I took a short rest at the infirmary. I was thinking of returning to the classroom now, but…"

"Is that right? However, we still have not found Miss Maria. It is dangerous to sit in such a place by yourself. Perhaps I could walk you back to the classroom?"

"Th-Thank you very much…"

With that, the president held out his hand. But it was then that a thought flitted into my mind. *What is he even doing here?* The academy was in the middle of class time, and I was the only student who'd been at the infirmary.

So yeah… what is the president doing here? I should ask him. I craned my neck, looking up at the president. His head full of red hair, now illuminated by the sun's rays, almost seemed to be sparkling.

That was it. Suddenly… a memory resurfaced from the depths of my mind.

"The hidden character route was really something, you know…? Unexpectedly difficult!" Acchan said, once again with that self-satisfied smile of hers. She continued on, despite knowing that I hated spoilers for the game's scenarios.

"He's quite a dangerous person, you know? With Dark Magic! If you succeed in the route, he spends happy days with the protagonist… but if you fail… the protagonist, her friends, and everyone in the student council… die. Everyone will be killed by this hidden character! A terrible Bad End, isn't it? Ah, also, he has a head full of red hair and grey eyes—"

Yes... it was exactly like I had heard from Acchan. The hidden character, and the endings that awaited...

In other words, the dream yesterday was not impossible at all. A horrible ending in which the protagonist and everyone in the student council dies... did indeed exist.

I felt beads of cold sweat trickling down my back. *How could I have forgotten something so important...? I really, really am a fool...*

Red hair and grey eyes — just like the person standing in front of me and smiling gently. The student council president, Sirius Dieke. As expected, he was yet another person with impossibly high stats. He was popular too, of course.

This man before me was none other than the hidden character of *Fortune Lover*, and the one who wielded Dark Magic.

I couldn't believe that my gentle, dependable senior would do such horrible things... that he would murder Maria, the student council, and everyone I cared about...

But if Jeord was right about all this, then these recent incidents were caused by a Wielder of Darkness. And if my memories of my past life were accurate... then the president, Sirius Dieke, was the one who was behind all this.

Magic paid for with a human life — the Dark Arts.

"Lady Katarina... is something wrong?" Sirius asked, noticing that I remained frozen and seated, despite him now holding my outstretched hand. He had his usual friendly expression on his face. Could it really be him?

"...President, are you really a... Wielder of Darkness? And... what have you done with Maria...?" I spoke before I could stop myself.

But Sirius just frowned a little with concern. "...What is this all about...? Wielding Darkness?" His expression didn't suggest that he knew anything about it.

That's right... the very existence of Dark Magic was unknown by the masses. Even I hadn't known anything about it — not until I had that conversation with Jeord. Even if he did have Dark Magic in the original setting of Fortune Lover, the current reality might have been different.

After all, even my close friends had remarkably different personalities than they had in the game, so even the president himself could be different. The Wielder of Darkness could be someone else.

"Oh, of course... you wouldn't know, President. How could our kind student council president have Dark Magic, or do anything terrible to Maria...?" Again, I blurted out what I was thinking. There was no way such a gentle person could sacrifice someone to gain power. It was impossible.

With those thoughts in mind, I turned my eyes to Sirius again. But his gaze... was different. He looked at me with a coldness in his eyes that I had never seen before.

"President...?"

"Kind, huh... You always say that about me, don't you...?"

"...Of course... It's because you are a kind person, President..." I found my voice quivering under his cold gaze.

Upon hearing my answer... the president's expression twisted. "That's just an act. It's easier to get by if I pretend to be gentle and calm, you see? You all, the fools you are, were completely taken in by this little charade."

"Huh?!"

The corner of Sirius' lips curled up at my expression of shock. Soon, a smile surfaced, twisted and mocking. This was far from the usual charming smile he had on his face.

"On another note... just so you know. The one who took Maria Campbell was me. All because she realized something she was better off not knowing," Sirius said coldly. "And also, Katarina Claes... I hate you. A false altruist pretending to care about the lonely and ostracized! The more I look at you, the more disgusted I feel!"

In an instant, his tone became nasty. The words that left his lips dripped with hostility. Sirius tightened his grip on my hand, still held in his. It was starting to hurt.

"You know what...? You should just *fucking disappear!*"

The lonely and ostracized...? Pretending to care? I didn't understand what he was talking about. But from the blatant hostility in his tone, I could tell that Sirius despised me.

So... it was as I thought. He had been the one who had done something to Maria. Then... would he claim the lives of Maria, everyone on the council, everyone I cared for... just like the game?

I gazed into Sirius' grey eyes. There was no trace of his usual calm expression. His eyes were cold, chilling me to the bone. He himself admitted that he had kidnapped Maria... and that his gentle disposition was nothing more than a façade. His words dripped with hostility and hatred. But... why?

"...Are you... okay?" I asked, raising my free hand slowly to his face.

With his cold eyes and hateful words, Sirius stood before me. But in contrast to what he said, the only thing I could see on his face was… pain. Even now, he looked like he was about to burst into tears. His face was pale, as if he could collapse at any moment.

My fingers brushed against his cheek — his skin was ice-cold.

"…Y-You witch! That's enough! Don't pity me, don't get involved with me! Stay away! Don't look at me with that smile of yours…! Just… Just get out of my sight!" Sirius shouted, roughly knocking away my raised hand.

As he did so, I could feel a blanket of darkness slowly falling over me. Somehow, my consciousness started to fade…

"Sleep. Just like that. Until your life ends…" Sirius said disdainfully.

Through my fading sense of awareness, the last thing I saw was… Sirius' face, and the tears that flowed freely from his eyes.

★★★★★★★★★★

"The tea that you brew has such a gentle flavor to it," my mother said, a calm smile on her face as she slowly patted me on the head.

Those were calm and happy days. However, that happiness was suddenly taken from me… and in an unimaginably hideous fashion.

That was when I swore. I swore that I would exact my revenge on those who had snatched my happiness away from me. That I would take everything they had — their reputation… their lives… everything.

I am the only son of Marquess Dieke — Sirius Dieke. At least, that is the name I have now.

As I had magical aptitude, I enrolled at the Academy of Magic on my fifteenth birthday. My high magical and academic skills soon came to light, and I was chosen to be part of the prestigious student council. In doing so, I brought honor to the Dieke family.

I first heard the name of that individual upon crossing paths with my old childhood friend, Nicol Ascart, at the Academy of Magic. The last time I had seen Nicol, he had barely turned ten. Now, five years later, I had run into him again.

However, Nicol had changed in those five years. I remembered him as a youth with eyes that reflected a perpetual sense of loneliness. Now, however, there was a sparkle in his gaze — not a single bit of loneliness was reflected within those jet-black eyes.

It was a pity, honestly, given that I had felt a sense of camaraderie with this boy with the lonely eyes. It did not take long for me to discover the name of the individual who had caused Nicol to change in this particular way.

"Katarina Claes." The daughter of the Claes family, and fiancée to Prince Jeord, third prince of the kingdom. The once silent and stoic Nicol often spoke of this girl. The more he spoke of her, the more his usual unchanging expression began to waver.

If I had to guess, the one who had taken away the loneliness in Nicol's eyes was none other than this girl.

In the spring of the next year, I was elected as student council president... and that was when she appeared before me.

From all that I had heard from Nicol, I had assumed that she was some sort of impossibly beautiful saint. Upon actually meeting Katarina Claes, however, it dawned upon me that she was a normal girl without any special traits, and she did not leave much of an impression on me.

Although she did possess somewhat attractive features, another girl elected to the council this year, Maria Campbell, was much more attractive in that regard. In addition, Katarina was not particularly smart, nor was she gifted with strong magical aptitude.

If I were to phrase it frankly, all Katarina Claes seemed to be was Prince Jeord's fiancée, and the daughter of Duke Claes. It seemed like she had nothing to offer beyond her station.

However, this relatively normal and unimpressive girl was respected and much-loved by her peers — said peers all being skilled and capable individuals, newly elected to the council.

That was also why they had leveled a threat against the lecturers and teachers: "If Katarina is not allowed free entry into the student council chambers, we will all rescind our nominations to the council," they said.

What exactly was so special, so desirable in this plain girl? Mysterious as it may have been, I didn't give her much of a second thought — none of this would matter as long as she did not interfere with my revenge.

For the sake of executing my revenge, I had to maintain my act as the reliable and calm student council president. I would, of course, have to get along with the new council members to some degree. To that end, I had to be kind and pleasant enough to this Katarina that they all loved so much.

It was with this thought in mind that I brewed some tea for Katarina Claes that day. It was nothing more than a hollow gesture.

"The tea that you brew has such a gentle flavor to it, President," Katarina Claes said with a peaceful smile as she raised the cup to her lips.

I felt a wave of unrest spread over my being at her words... and her smile. So much so that the mask I had worn for years almost seemed ready to shatter at that very moment.

Up until now, the other student council members only had the usual pleasantries to say about the tea I brewed. That it was "delicious," or something along those lines. However, there was only one other person in my entire life... who had said that the tea I brewed had a "gentle flavor."

To make things worse, the way she smiled was much like how that person used to smile. I felt something deep in my chest stirring. With my previously unwavering resolve shaken, I found myself not knowing how to appropriately deal with Katarina.

The deception that I had steadily maintained across the years allowed me to interact with her somewhat normally. Ever since this incident, however, all of my interactions with Katarina Claes only served to spread even more shockwaves across my being, dampening my resolve.

On the day that everything was taken from me, I had sworn to have my revenge. I would put on this calm and gentle mask of mine, pursue academic achievements, and continue deceiving everyone else around me... all the while using the Dark Magic that I had obtained. I would weave plan after plan, preparing for the inevitable.

I gathered funds, fabricated crimes and evidence. The day would soon come when I could exact my revenge on those who had snatched away my happiness all those years ago. However... I found myself unable to continue on with my tasks. Not after I met this... Katarina Claes.

For the sake of my revenge, I was capable of doing anything, even if it meant dirtying my own hands. Up until now, I had not felt a single shred of regret or hesitation. Never once had my resolve been shaken. And yet... and yet.

When I looked into those azure eyes and that smile on her face — I could feel my heart twisting and swirling like a maelstrom.

There was a girl by the name of Campbell on the student council. Maria Campbell. She was a commoner, and yet a Wielder of Light. A special girl.

Maria was proficient in both academics and magic. She had a good head on her shoulders, and a most charming visage that easily captured the hearts of all those who gazed upon her. A truly blessed girl.

Even so, she often had a certain look of loneliness in her eyes. That look was exactly like the one Nicol used to have. I felt a sense of camaraderie towards this girl, too.

However, she changed. Somewhere along the line, the aura of loneliness around her being all but vanished — and soon I saw her with Katarina even outside the council chambers, as if they were the best of friends.

Ever since then, Maria's eyes seemed to chase after Katarina. Should their eyes ever meet, she would smile ever so faintly, as if overcome by joy.

CHAPTER 4: THE APPROACHING FOOTSTEPS OF DESTRUCTION

Katarina Claes was surrounded by the smiles and laughter of many. She was the one who brought this sparkle to Nicol and Maria's eyes. They were happy just being by her side. Looking at her then, I finally started to understand why Nicol seemed to view her as some sort of saint.

My heart, however, was filled with a vortex of emotions every time I cast my eyes upon her... so much so that the mask I had developed, this deception that I had maintained for all these years... sometimes began to crumble.

"Why are you bothering with someone like that? Continue the preparations for your revenge!" another voice within me said, as I felt my heart ravaged by the very sight of that girl.

Now that it had come to this... it appeared that I could no longer disregard the existence of Katarina Claes.

It was pure coincidence that I witnessed the bullying of Maria Campbell. Although I knew that she was the target of petty bullying by students who were jealous of her, this was the first time I had seen it in person.

As the student council president, there was no way Sirius Dieke wouldn't intervene. And so I did what I had to do, giving a stern warning to the nobles bullying her.

"Are you alright?" I asked.

"Thank you very much. I am alright," Maria said, as if the experience had not bothered her in the slightest.

Even so, I couldn't help but feel baffled and exasperated at the sheer petty foolishness of these young lords and ladies. Maria Campbell was a commoner, and as such had a relatively low social standing in the academy. Even so, she was a Wielder of Light. If anything, she should be a valuable presence — one of the rare few blessed with Light Magic in this kingdom.

155

In fact, the Magical Ministry had long since had its eye on Maria, ever since she came to the academy. Blessed with Light Magic and high magical capabilities, Maria Campbell was sure to obtain a high position in the ministry upon graduation.

To bully and harass someone like Maria, who would be accepted into an association that held the reins of power to the kingdom only second to the king himself... it was plain to see that they would pay for their crimes one day. And yet, they did not realize this... the utter fools.

It was then that the idea struck my mind. Why not frame Katarina Claes? Frame her for all the bullying and harassment that Maria Campbell had experienced.

If I succeeded in this endeavor, even Katarina Claes, the daughter of Duke Claes, wouldn't be able to get away unscathed. If everything went according to plan, Katarina might even disappear from the academy... and disappear from my sight. If I could do that, my heart would no longer waver. My resolve would never again be shaken.

With that in mind, the rest of the plan was simple. All I had to do was investigate what kind of bullying Maria was subject to, and then have Katarina do the exact same things. To that end, I had to control Katarina with my Dark Magic, and then have her bully Maria in those specific ways.

My plan, however, did not come to fruition.

Dark Magic was said to be able to dominate the hearts and minds of others. However, the means by which one would attain such powers, as well as the dangerous nature of Dark Magic itself, meant that its very existence was hidden from the public at large.

In spite of all this, Dark Magic was not omnipotent — far from it. One could not exactly control the hearts of others however they pleased. Erasing certain memories, or snatching away one's consciousness for a set period of time... that much was possible. Dark Magic, however, was not capable of creating something that was not already there.

For instance, Dark Magic could not make someone hate what they loved... nor could it make them suddenly adore what they detested. What it could do was cause the seeds of jealousy, envy, or even hatred, to slowly grow — and this would eventually incite the individual to act. However, if the person in question did not have any jealousy, envy, or hatred in their heart in the first place, nothing could be done.

I had assumed that I could simply amplify the envy in Katarina's heart. Sooner or later, this would cause her to bully Maria. But of course... Katarina did not have the slightest feelings of envy towards Maria. I could not amplify something that was not there. In the end, I was unable to incite Katarina to bully her friend.

As a result, I had to change my plans... In the end, all I could do was take advantage of the envy and hatred of those noble girls who bore ill will towards Katarina, provide them with fabricated circumstantial evidence, and then have them publicly blame her for all the bullying. Even that took quite some effort to pull off.

I made sure to lure away Katarina's friends, her dependable knights, on the day of the incident. While she did seem cornered initially, her supporters came to her rescue earlier than I had anticipated, and my plan ended in failure. The false evidence that I had crafted was immediately dismissed by the friends who loved her so. Even Maria Campbell, who had indeed been bullied and harassed, stood up for her, claiming that "Lady Katarina would never do such a thing."

Honestly speaking, my inability to dominate Katarina's mind meant that this plan had a low chance of success to begin with. But for it to fail to this extent...

I made those girls forget, and modified the memories of all those involved in preoccupying members of the student council during that lunch break. As a result, there was no way anyone could trace this incident to me.

I hadn't suffered any backlash for this failure. The plan had a low rate of success — I suppose nothing could be done about it. That was when the other voice in me spoke out.

"There was no way that you, wise as you are, would not have anticipated this. You knew from the start that this plan would not work. Were you really serious about getting rid of that annoying girl?"

Was I really serious? Was I? Of course... I had to erase her. I had to remove her from my sight.

Yes, that was exactly it. That girl caused my resolve to waver. She must be made to disappear. That was why I came up with this plan in the first place.

However, I couldn't help but feel a deep sense of contradiction. Even though my plan had failed, I somehow felt... relieved?

I gazed at Katarina from a distance. There she was, surrounded by her friends, smiling happily. With a complex mixture of disappointment and relief in my heart, I plodded back to the council chambers.

With this, the curtains should have been drawn on this event. Upon returning to the council chambers, I set about arranging some documents... and it was then that she appeared.

Maria Campbell. The one who had so magnificently shielded Katarina moments ago, the very same one who had foiled my plans… and the only Wielder of Light in the Academy of Magic.

Lunch break was already over. Why would she be here at this time…? My question, however, was soon answered. Her face pale, Maria began to speak.

"I noticed some time ago, President… that you were occasionally glaring at Lady Katarina. I assumed that I was just imagining things… but then I was thinking about what just happened. I did not want to think that you were involved in this incident, President. And so I thought I could come to check on you. Well then… what exactly are those things?"

"Whatever are you talking about, Miss Campbell…? What do you mean by 'incident'…? Did something happen to Lady Katarina?" I responded, a fake expression of worry on my face.

To think that I had let my mask slip and openly glared at Katarina a few times… what a colossal mistake. Even so, Maria didn't have any evidence to back up her words. All I had to do was erase that memory.

"You don't know…? But that is impossible. You must be connected in some way… after all, it's the same. That black aura around you… looks exactly like that black presence that was drifting over the noble ladies harassing Lady Katarina!"

"What?!" My eyes opened wide, in spite of myself. A black presence, an aura… was she referring to the presence of Dark Magic?

No one had ever noticed a thing, even though I had been using my magic all this time. I took it for granted that no one could detect my Dark Magic. Could it be…

Ah. Because she is a Wielder of Light. It was a reasonable assumption. I hadn't encountered a single Wielder of Light, not since first obtaining my Dark Magic powers.

Dark and Light were pure opposites. Maria Campbell and her Light Magic… was it because of this that she was able to perceive my powers?

Maria, with her stern expression, appeared to have seen right through me. Now that it had come to this… continuing the charade would be difficult. In that case…

"Ha. Haha. As expected of a Wielder of Light. That's right. I was the mastermind behind this entire incident. All so that I could erase that irritating girl…"

"What?!" Maria, frozen to the spot with her eyes wide, could hardly react as I walked towards her slowly. After all, Dark Magic could not activate without contact. I placed a single hand on Maria's shoulder.

"But you see… you need not worry your pretty little head."

I would simply erase this, and several other memories from Maria's mind. In a few seconds, she would forget about this conversation… or so I thought.

"Well then, Miss Maria. If you don't return to the classrooms soon, lessons will start without you."

"…What are you talking about, President…? We're not done here," Maria said, suspicion and surprise written all over her features.

…Could it be?! I let my Dark Magic slither across Maria once more. However…

"What have you been trying to do… just now?" Maria said, with that same expression. It would appear that she was unaffected by the Dark Arts.

Wielders of Light must be immune to the Dark Arts... I won't be able to erase her memories...! In that case... I cannot simply allow her to leave.

"President... why would you... Lady Katarina..."

If magic didn't work, a physical tactic would. Soon, Maria was unconscious. She had discovered something that she was better off not knowing. With me unable to erase her memories, I could not simply allow her to return to Katarina and the rest.

And so, I carried the still unconscious Maria to a hidden chamber in the academy grounds. I had planned and schemed so well up until now. This was my biggest failure.

All this... was because I got involved with Katarina Claes.

"*That girl is a hindrance. Erase her, now. Quickly!*" the voice within me demanded.

Maria's disappearance was soon known to Katarina and her friends. Before long, they started searching for her in earnest.

The existence of a hidden chamber in the academy was only known to a few in the Dieke family. Surely, they would not easily discover where Maria was hidden. Even so, I couldn't simply lock her up forever.

Since then, I had tried many times to alter or erase Maria's memories with the Dark Arts. Maria, however, showed no sign of succumbing. I was now at a loss.

It was then that the voice within me spoke once more. "*Well then... you might as well just kill her. What better way to silence her once and for all?*"

I took some time during a self-study period to check on how Maria was doing on the fourth day of her confinement. Assuming that the Dark Arts could potentially work on her should her spirits be dampened, I continued observing her — and yet, despite being cooped up in a dark room for an extended period of time, Maria's will was steadfast.

Irritated at the deadlock I had found myself in, I made my way back to the classrooms... and that was when I saw a familiar figure seated on a bench in the open courtyard. It was the culprit herself, the one responsible for putting me into this mess... Katarina Claes.

"Lady Katarina? Whatever are you doing here?"

Katarina turned around, surprised by a sudden voice calling out to her from behind. "Ah... I was feeling a little sick, and so I took a short rest at the infirmary. I was thinking of returning to the classroom now, but..." Indeed, she did look rather pale.

"Is that right? However, we still have not found Miss Maria. It is dangerous to sit in such a place by yourself. Perhaps I could walk you back to the classroom?"

As Sirius Dieke, the student council president, I had no choice but to say those words to her. I extended my hand to the seated Katarina.

"Th-Thank you very much..."

As Katarina placed her hand into mine with a smile, I could feel my heart wavering, now more than ever before. I couldn't help but feel uncomfortable in this open, warm courtyard, so lovingly caressed by the sun's rays.

I wanted to quickly return to the classrooms. For some reason, however... Katarina was now frozen and unmoving, her hand still in mine.

"Lady Katarina... is something wrong?"

Her azure eyes stared into mine. And then...

"...President, are you really a... Wielder of Darkness? And... what have you done with Maria...?"

Although it was a huge shock to hear those words all of a sudden, I was able to quickly recover, in no small part due to the continuous deception I had maintained across the years. I pretended to know nothing of Dark Magic, assuming an expression of confusion and feigned worry.

Katarina lowered her head slightly, as if lost in thought. *Why would she say something like this, all of a sudden...? Has she known of the existence of Dark Magic from the very beginning, or has one of her faithful knights sniffed me out? Still, I can't be sure that's the case...*

Much like Maria, Katarina seemed somewhat unsure of herself. All I had to do was bluff my way out of this with smoke and mirrors... or at least, that was what I intended to do.

"Oh, of course... you wouldn't know, President. How could our kind student council president have Dark Magic, or do anything terrible to Maria...?" Katarina mumbled, more to herself than anyone else.

Upon hearing those words, I could feel it: a cracking sensation deep inside of me. Before I even realized it, the calm, composed mask of Sirius Dieke, painstakingly maintained across all these years, had been ruthlessly torn off my face.

"President...?" Katarina said, looking at me, shaken.

"Kind, huh... You always say that about me, don't you...?"

"...Of course... It's because you are a kind person, President..."

Still the same words even after my mask has been torn off, Katarina... What a foolish girl you are.

163

"That's just an act. It's easier to get by if I pretend to be gentle and calm, you see? You all, the fools you are, were completely taken in by this little charade."

"Huh?!"

I allowed a menacing smile to spread across my face to ridicule the wide-eyed Katarina. "On another note... just so you know. The one who took Maria Campbell was me. All because she realized something she was better off not knowing."

I went on, "And also, Katarina Claes... I hate you. A false altruist pretending to care about the lonely and ostracized! The more I look at you, the more disgusted I feel!"

It was as if a dam had burst within me. The words continued pouring out, each faster than the last.

"You know what...? You should just *fucking disappear!*"

I hurled my hostile, hateful words at the girl. With this, even Katarina should be sufficiently terrified... perhaps she would even throw some hurtful insults my way, or maybe even regard me with hateful eyes. That was what I expected.

"...Are you... okay?" Katarina's response was a question. In her eyes was... worry. I didn't know why, but she seemed worried for me.

Why...? Why is she looking at me with those eyes, again...? Did she not hear what I just said? I clearly recall claiming that I was the one who had kidnapped Maria.

And then Katarina slowly raised her free hand, reaching out to my face, gently brushing my cheek. Like she was... empathizing with me.

Why, why, why...?! Why do you not fear me, why do you not hate me...? Don't look at me with those eyes!

I immediately knocked aside her warm hand. "...Y-You witch! That's enough! Don't pity me, don't get involved with me! Stay away! Don't look at me with that smile of yours...! Just... Just get out of my sight!"

If I stared into those azure eyes any longer... If she approached me again... If she smiled at me just one more time... I felt like I could no longer continue being who I needed to be.

I once swore that I would do anything for the sake of my revenge. Now, more than ever, I could feel my resolve dangerously shaking.

"Erase this woman..." the voice within me said. Obeying, I allowed Dark Magic to flow into Katarina's outstretched hand.

"Sleep. Just like that. Until your life ends..."

Katarina fell slowly, before my eyes, collapsing onto the ground. Having been spirited away into the land of dreams, she no longer had any free will. She would most likely sleep, and continue sleeping... until she died.

Now, finally... that annoying eyesore of a girl was gone. I would now be able to continue living my life for the sake of revenge... just as I had done before. My resolve would no longer waver.

Or so I thought... *Then why? Why has this vortex of emotion in my heart not calmed down in the slightest?* In fact, the sight of Katarina sleeping only served to intensify this feeling.

A strange, water-like fluid began falling from my eyes. *What, exactly... is this?*

★★★★★★★★★

I was seated in a dark, dim room, on a chair next to a bed. Filled with unease, I stood up once more, reaching out towards the bed's pillow. How many times had I done this?

I could only sigh with some degree of relief as I affirmed the temperature and steady breathing of the girl who was peacefully sleeping in a bed in the student dormitory.

To me, Anne Shelley, the girl in the bed was the most important person to me. She was Lady Katarina Claes.

Although she still drew breath, her body would not move an inch. The young miss merely continued her deep sleep. What if the warmth started to fade from her body…? Such thoughts would cross my mind every ten minutes or so, filling me with a deep worry. Once again, I would get up to ascertain her temperature and breathing.

It had been two days since Lady Katarina had fallen into such a state. I had been by her bedside all this time. I found myself unable to sleep… nor did I have much of an appetite. Although my colleagues had offered to take my place so that I may rest, time and time again, I just could not allow them to. It did not feel like something I could do. Should anything ever happen to Lady Katarina in my absence… No. I could not possibly leave her side.

I held Lady Katarina's hand in mine, looking at her serene face. The boisterous, rowdy young miss, who would often kick off her blankets and pillows in her sleep… was now lying motionless. I simply could not shake the feeling that this was disturbingly abnormal.

How could this happen…?

It was two days ago that Lady Katarina was found collapsed in the courtyard near the school buildings, when the sun was almost ready to set. She was then carried back to her room in the dormitory.

According to Prince Jeord, the young miss was unwell that morning, and had been escorted to the infirmary to rest. Later, when he attempted to visit her, he was told that Lady Katarina had already returned to her lessons.

Thinking that he had missed her, Prince Jeord returned to the classrooms, but the young miss was nowhere to be seen. In a panic, he searched for her everywhere, before finally locating her, collapsed in a corner of the courtyard.

No matter how many times he called her name, Lady Katarina never responded. Prince Jeord immediately brought her to the infirmary, and promptly summoned some doctors to tend to her. "She is merely asleep," the prince was told.

Afterwards, the prince continued to call her name, but Lady Katarina continued to slumber — and so she was brought to her personal quarters. Again, a doctor was summoned, only for the prince to be told that she was "sleeping."

Unable to bear with Lady Katarina's unnatural state of stupor any longer, Prince Jeord exercised his royal rights as the third prince to call one of the most acclaimed doctors in the kingdom. Armed with a magnificent moustache, the visibly senior doctor was responsible for the health and well-being of the royal family itself — he was one of the very best in the kingdom, if not all the lands. I had hoped that this doctor would be able to do something. I sincerely hoped that this would be so, and yet...

"It is most unfathomable, honestly. She does not seem physically unwell — this much I know, from all the examinations I have done. Perhaps she may awaken immediately... perhaps she may never open her eyes again."

"What, then... would happen to Katarina if she continued sleeping like this...?" Prince Jeord inquired with a grave expression.

The doctor could only give an apologetic answer. "...If the young lady continues to sleep, Your Highness... she will be unable to have any water or food. If this circumstance is prolonged... I fear she will lose her life."

"*What*?! Impossible! How could something like this...?!" Even the usually calm and collected Master Keith momentarily lost his cool, relentlessly demanding answers from the aged doctor.

WHAM!

My eyes instinctively followed the sound of the impact. Prince Jeord, who only ever had a smile on his face... Prince Jeord, who never once raised his voice... had his fist up against the wall.

Lady Mary, too, had become completely pale. I could almost hear her rattling as she shivered. She seemed ready to faint at any moment.

Prince Alan's expression was one that was foreign to me. His features were incredibly stiff, as if his entire being was dedicated to maintaining a stoic expression.

Lady Sophia was simply standing where she was, as tear after tear dropped down from her eyes, opened wide in shock. Not a single wail escaped her lips.

And Master Nicol... his fists were clenched so tight, it almost seemed like his skin was changing color.

From where I was seated, I could only watch over all of the young miss' friends in her room... I, too, would immediately collapse should my determination waver. Lady Katarina may very well lose her life. I could feel myself impaled by the notion, sinking slowly into despair at the thought of such a possibility.

After this, many other doctors were summoned to her bedside. None of the doctors, however, understood the reason for the young miss' slumber. Not a single one could wake her. Occasionally, a rare Wielder of Light would show up. Even so... the outcome remained unchanged. A day, and then another... and yet, there was no sign that Lady Katarina was any closer to waking.

She was the one who had given me purpose. The one who allowed a tool such as myself to once again become human. The most important person to me in the world.

As I strongly held her hand in my own, I prayed silently. *I have already decided that I would live my life by your side. So please... Lady Katarina, I beg of you. Please... please do not leave us.*

"*No, not at all. Please don't worry about this, Your Highness. It is a small wound, one that can be easily hidden with my bangs! There is no problem at all.*"

Much time had passed since that day. Seven years since the girl before me had smiled and said those words. My dearest fiancée... Katarina Claes.

My existence was all but forgotten at the castle, and all I had were days of boredom. But then, this mysterious girl suddenly appeared before me. With her strange words and amusing actions, I found myself slowly drawn in. The more time I spent with Katarina, the more I realized that the world before me — that once grey, drab world — was now filled with vibrant color.

All I had known was tedium. I knew nothing of happiness... or the very notion of fun. I knew nothing of such things, and yet Katarina taught me all of it. Even jealousy, sadness... emotions that I surely would not have felt, had I not met her.

Seven years had passed since our fateful meeting. I could no longer bear the thought of returning to that grey, drab world... a world without Katarina.

In the beginning, it was nothing more than a calculated strategy, a political engagement. However, before I knew it, I had come to love Katarina Claes more than anyone else in the world.

Alas, she was naturally born a charmer, and many would flock to her... but I had long since made up my mind. Now that she was in my hands, I would never let go.

And yet. How could this be...? I knew nothing of Katarina being exposed to danger. I was unable to protect her. All I could feel were strong pangs of regret and guilt. I blamed myself for my failure.

Perhaps the Dark Arts were responsible for Katarina's catatonic state. Such was my assumption, and I had even summoned Wielders of Light... to no avail. We knew nothing.

"Perhaps one with an even stronger magical aptitude, one also blessed with Light Magic... they may have some answers." So I was told. But of course, the only individual with such qualifications was Maria Campbell, and she herself was still missing. The situation was most dire.

I could only curse my own helplessness as I slammed my fist straight into the wall.

"Keith, we are brother and sister, you know. You should call me Big Sister!"

That was what she said to me, with that smile on her face. I couldn't believe it had already been seven years.

Even so, I remember all of it as if it were yesterday. Of how I was abused, called a monster… Of how I would hug my knees to my chest in a dark room, living my lonely life. And yet she turned to me with a smile, soothing me with a warm hand on my back.

"I'll stay with you forever!" she said.

My adopted sister, Katarina Claes, was a ray of light into my world of darkness. Her warmth, and her gentle smile… as if the love she had for me was more than what a sister would have for her brother. The most precious, most important person to me in the world.

I had always been with her. And we were supposed to be together — from here on out, as well. I had no intention of handing her over, not even to her fiancé, Prince Jeord.

I had sworn to protect her with these very hands. To that end, I had put my entire being into mastering the sword, honing my magic, and even the appropriate etiquette one would display as a noble. All for the sake of protecting Katarina.

How could this have happened? Why was I not with her then…? Even though I'd sworn to protect her…? I could not hold back the regret in my heart.

After I became the adopted son of the Claes family at the age of eight, whenever things were hard, Katarina was always there, with that gentle smile of hers…

All I wished now was to see that smile again. I could not bear losing her.

I raised a hand to my shoulder, trying to quell the tremors that assaulted my body.

★★★★★★★★★

"You have a green thumb, Mary! Maybe even green hands too, ha! Yes! You have a real talent. You're a special and wonderful person!"

Even now, I remember clearly… the day she held my hands, so tightly in hers. I was a coward. Always with my eyes downcast, always running. I hated myself.

But then, Katarina Claes said that I was a special, wonderful person. I was so very happy.

My older sisters claimed that I was "filthy." They hated my eyes and hair — both the color of burnt sienna. Katarina, however, said she liked them. She said that they were pretty.

I put my all into becoming the ideal noble lady — one who could proudly stand by Katarina's side. Honestly… there were so many times when things had gone wrong, when obstructions to my goal had arisen. But because Katarina was with me, because she was fond of me, because she said that I was important to her, I was able to overcome all these challenges.

The only reason why I am the Mary Hunt I am now… is all because I've been allowed to be by Katarina's side. Even now, and into the future, I longed to stand by her forever. Katarina was important to me. So important that it made me want to snatch her away from her fiancé.

And yet... when I gazed upon her as she was now, it was like all life had left her. The sight of Katarina, sleeping so peacefully, flooded my mind. I could feel my vision going dark... but I held on. I held on like my life depended on it.

There is no way I would just lose consciousness like this... No! I will not stand for it! For I am Katarina's dearest friend, Mary Hunt! I am NOTHING like those weak-willed noble ladies one would so casually find in this kingdom!

I have to do everything I can for Katarina...!

I righted my posture, raising my head.

★★★★★★★★★

"The same goes for you, Prince Alan. There are skills that you can be proud of too. It's just a matter of... individual strengths and weaknesses."

I'd always been compared to my twin brother. I'd all but given up, and then she says that to me. With those blue eyes of hers, she turned to me and looked right at me... and never once let up in those matches we had. Katarina Claes, the girl who climbed up trees like a crazy monkey.

I'd lost myself to the voices around me, trapped in my own delusions. She was the one who snapped me back to reality. It was only after meeting her that I could finally let that chip on my shoulder go.

She was always looking straight ahead, never lying. I felt comfortable and peaceful when I was with her. So... I just thought I'd keep standing by her side like I always did.

But then... this happens. The thought of losing Katarina gave me a kind of fear I didn't know I could feel. And that was when I noticed just how important she was to me. And I realized that I wanted to be with her forever.

But I was stupid. I was dense. I only realized my own feelings when we were on the verge of losing her. She was my brother's fiancée, so I knew there was no way my wish would come true. But... I still wanted to be by her side, as much as I was allowed. There was no way I could bear losing her right now.

I had to do something... anything. I had to help Katarina.

★★★★★★★★★

"You really are blessed, Master Nicol, to have such amazing parents, and a cute younger sister."

The day she said those words to me. Those words, that smile. I could never forget them.

Everyone had simply decided that I was unfortunate, and that I was to be pitied... because of my important family. *"But I am fortunate."* No matter how many times I repeated this, no one would understand. And I felt that this was how it would always be, and that I should simply give up.

Katarina Claes, however... understood. My heart, which was once blanketed by frustration, was now instead cradled with warmth. From that day onwards, Katarina was a special person to me.

I was never very good at interacting with others. Often, I would turn my gaze away from theirs. But Katarina always looked at me with her clear eyes. She always faced me with a smile that was as bright as the sun. It was most calming to be with her.

Katarina Claes was fiancée of my childhood friend Jeord, third prince of the kingdom. I did not have to think much about it to

know that we could be together. I understood that much. However…
I wished to spend as much time as possible with her, at least within
permissible limits.

"*An accomplished young man like you will surely become a favored
candidate for the position of chancellor.*" That was what everyone
around me said. However… what could I do in this situation? I hated
myself for being so helpless. I could not even protect one person —
the most important person to me.

So much for the lauded chancellor candidate… I tightened my
balled fists once more. I could feel my nails digging in, and the
sensation of blood slowly dripping from my palm.

★★★★★★★★★

"*I think your silky white hair is beautiful. I think your ruby-red,
sparkling eyes are beautiful. I think… you… are beautiful.*"

I was different. I… looked different. People would gossip… say
that I was cursed, or that I was disgusting.

But then… this girl said that I was "beautiful." She then held
out her hand and asked… "*Would you like to be my friend?*"

At first, I thought she was just playing along… showing me a
dream that was convenient at the time. But… that was no dream. For
the first time in my life I made a friend. She turned to me, smiling
gently.

From the moment I met the girl known as Katarina Claes, my
world changed completely. I felt like I was propelled out of the dark
room that I had confined myself into… and that I was now under
the warm rays of the sun. Finally, I had obtained the happiness I had
only dreamed of before… in my fantasies and thoughts, between
those walls.

I wanted these days to go on forever. That was my sincere wish... then why, why did this happen? For those two days, tears would start flowing from my eyes the very moment I lost my focus. I cried and cried... until I felt like I had used up all the water I could possibly contain in my body. Even so, the tears simply kept flowing.

It had been two days since Katarina had suddenly collapsed. I visited her chambers countless times. So many times I called out to her... but I could not see even the slightest hint of a reaction. My heart ached at the sight of Katarina continuing to sleep soundlessly.

I really just... wanted to stay by Katarina's bedside. However... my brother disagreed, dragging me back to my room. "That would simply not do, Sophia," he said.

Now that we were physically apart... even now, I could feel a deep sense of unease... the thought of losing Katarina. For the past two days, she had been visited by a variety of doctors... but none of them could wake Katarina from her slumber, despite their many methods and attempts.

If she kept sleeping like this, Katarina could very well lose her life... When I heard those words, they just... did not seem real. The sudden declaration pierced my reality.

No matter the kind of doctor that visited, not a single one of them had a concrete answer. Now, two days had passed... and those words slowly started feeling more and more real.

If this went on, I would really lose Katarina... I would never be able to see her smile ever again! *No... I cannot accept that! I don't want to lose her!* The thought surged strongly into my mind. It was then that I heard it.

"That's right! I won't accept it! I don't want to lose her, not again!" A voice suddenly called out. It was a voice that I had no recollection of — and yet... it felt so, so nostalgic.

Surprised, I turned, looking this way and that around me. I had asked the servants to stand down, so there was no one but me, alone in my dormitory room.

"After all this time, we've met again... I don't want to lose her! This time, for sure, I have to help her! So don't just sit and cry in a place like this! Bring me to her side! Quickly!"

It was like the strange voice came from deep within myself. Guided by the mysterious voice, I stood up and slowly walked in the direction of Katarina's quarters.

"Lady Sophia?! Whatever are you doing here at this hour?" Katarina's maid asked, involuntarily raising her voice at the sight of me.

But of course she would say that. It was already this deep into the night, and I had visited Katarina's chambers without even asking for permission. Under normal circumstances, this was something that would never, ever be done... it was an action that went against societal common sense.

Even so... for some reason, I felt like I simply had to do it... Like the mysterious voice within me instructed me to.

"...Lady Katarina..." I approached the bed, clasping her hands in both of mine. As I did so, I saw my brother approach from the corner of my eye. I suppose word of my social faux pas had already reached him...

"Sophia... calm yourself." He placed his hands on my shoulders, trying to guide me back to my room... However, I refused.

Perhaps word of my stubbornness spread quickly... but before I knew it, Prince Jeord, Prince Alan, Master Keith, and Lady Mary were all present. Regardless, I continued holding onto Katarina's hand. I refused to let go. I was not going to move from this place.

I held her hand against my forehead, closed my eyes... and prayed — with all of my heart. "Please... I beg of you. Please help Lady Katarina."

As I did so, I felt like I could see the face of a young girl in the darkness. She had black hair and dark eyes. There was no way I could have known her. And yet... something about her was so, so nostalgic.

"Okay, leave it to me! I'll definitely bring her back! All you have to do is continue calling out to her from where you are!" the girl said, her gaze filled with resolute strength. And then, as suddenly as she appeared... she was gone.

★★★★★★★★★

It had been two days since I put Katarina Claes to sleep with the Dark Arts. Try as they might, her knights could not wake her.

After all, Dark Magic could only be dispelled by the one who was responsible for casting it in the first place. If Katarina continued to slumber as she did... she would surely die.

That, precisely, was what I had wished for all along. Then... why? For some reason, my heart refused to calm itself. When I thought about how Katarina would be gone, just like that, I felt my chest tightening. It was hard to breathe.

...No. I don't want to lose her... I have to dispel the Dark Arts I used on her.

"What foolishness you speak of!" the voice within me said, rage evident in its voice. *"That girl is nothing more than an obstacle to your revenge! Those who dare get in the way of your revenge have to be erased... there is no other way!"*

The more I hesitated, the more upset the voice within me grew.

"You've LIVED your very life for revenge! To utterly destroy those who took your mother's life, the ones who used you as a tool! Were you not going to send them to the depths of hell? Was that not your reason for living? Have you forgotten your mother's last words?!"

Yes... the last words of the mother I loved so much. The very last thing that left her lips. That was my reason for living. "...Please, avenge me..."

I had no other reason to live. All I needed was my revenge.

"How long are you going to sleep, you fool daughter?!"

As that thunderous voice shook me from my sleep, I felt my blanket being pulled away.

"...H-Huh? What?" Shocked, I squinted in the sudden bright light.

The person who had pulled my blanket away was now glaring at me. "Don't you 'what' me! How many times have I called for you and tried to wake you? You're going to be late for school again!"

"...Wha...? M-Mother...?"

"'Mother'? ...What's gotten into you? Are you unwell? Did you oversleep and lose your mind?"

"...Huh? What? Ah... G-Good morning, Mom." I stared up at my mom, who was now standing over me with an intimidating pose. With her downward-slanting, beady eyes, she kind of reminded me of a fox.

"Aren't you already a high schooler? Can't you fix your own hair and tidy your own uniform?" she said, making me sit up.

I caught sight of myself in the mirror. My face was like my mother's — fox-like, but somewhat normal-looking. *Why do I feel... like something's off? Is this really my face? Hmm... perhaps, at one point, but my face now is more...*

"What are you doing, still lazing around?! You're really going to be late if you don't hurry it up!"

Mom's screeching voice prompted me to look up at the clock. She was right — time was almost up.

I quickly jumped up from my bed and went through the motions to prepare myself for school. I took off my pajamas, jumped into my school uniform, doused my face with water, and then my preparations were complete.

"At the very least, do something about that rat's nest," Mom said. But my hair was stubborn, and no matter what I did, there was a cowlick that simply wouldn't go away. I decided to leave it.

But... my hair was different now. It was long and flowing. Every morning, Anne would help me prepare for the day by brushing me... *Huh? My hair now? What does that even mean? What did Anne do...? Who's this Anne again?*

Hmm... I still feel like something's off. How weird. Something definitely isn't right. Am I forgetting something important?

Ah! It's this time already? I need to hurry! The minute hand of the clock seemed to move unnaturally fast the moment I took my eyes off it. I didn't have any time to sit around and think about things! I rushed to the living room as fast as I could.

My older brother, who was a university student, was elegantly eating his breakfast at the table. "Oh, good morning. When will you finally be able to wake up without having your blanket pulled off your sleepy self?" he said.

My other brother, who was a salaryman, had already set off for work. My father was gone to work too. Mom was standing next to my brother, who seemed to be amused. She quickly thrust a lunchbox in my general direction.

"Thanks!" A low rumbling in my stomach started as soon as the lunchbox was in my hands. My hunger got worse at the sight of the delicious meal that was laid out on the table, but I didn't have time to sit down and eat.

I scanned the table for something I could eat on the way... but there was nothing that would work. Left without a choice, I rummaged through the fridge for something that would fit in my mouth while I rode my bike. I finally found something and stuffed it in my mouth.

"Amf goin naw! Baai!" With a cheerful goodbye, I turned towards the front door. Then, I turned to look at my mom one more time before I left. For some reason, my brother was laughing uncontrollably behind her.

"Wait... what is that in your..." I guess Mom was saying something, but I didn't have time to listen. Ignoring her, I rushed out of the house and onto my bike in one swift motion.

As my cycling speed increased, I could hear my mom's voice calling out from behind me. "At least choose bread or something! Why is there a CUCUMBER in your mouth?!"

I munched on my breakfast cucumber while pedaling down the street. It was probably from Grandma's farm. It was definitely fresh and had a distinctive taste of its own, but it was kind of bland without any seasoning. I wished I had put some miso paste on it before hurrying to school.

With chunks of cucumber in my cheek, I endured the terrible howls and barks of the dog that lived near my house and somehow managed to pedal all the way to school, arriving just as the bells for the first lesson rang out.

I headed to the classroom quickly, and once I got nearby, I could hear some kind of ruckus. I figured that our homeroom teacher hadn't arrived yet.

"I made it! Safe!" I muttered, entering the classroom quietly through the back door.

"Unfortunately... you did not," my homeroom teacher said, glaring at me from his spot on the podium.

And so, for the terrible crime of being late for a few minutes, I was condemned to a lecture by my homeroom teacher during lunch break.

Halfway through lunch, the lecture ended. Deflated, I moped my way to Acchan's classroom. She had been a great otaku friend of mine ever since middle school. We were assigned to different classes in our second year of high school, but I made sure to visit her at lunch so that we could have our otaku talk. It was an important part of my daily life.

Acchan, seeing me come in so late, immediately said... "Let me guess. You were late, caught, and lectured again. Are you ever going to manage to get to school on time?" She seemed to have guessed at my unfortunate circumstances, but she sounded exasperated.

"I just stayed up a liiittle bit last night... and then couldn't get up this morning..."

My friend seemed even more exasperated in response. "Playing games deep into the night again? You really need to pay more attention to the time..."

"...Ugh... I just kinda got annoyed and kept going I guess..."

After getting into high school, I was introduced to otome games and was quickly hooked from my very first one. I was always like this when I got a new game; I'd always forget the time as I got engrossed in the gameplay.

"Seriously... Burning the midnight oil just for games? Did you at least make any progress in *Fortune Lover*?"

Fortune Lover was an otome game that I'd gotten recently, and the very same game that kept me up that night.

"Yeah... I was thinking I should try out the path of the arrogant prince. Alan's route!"

Alan was a potential love interest in the setting of *Fortune Lover*, known as the "arrogant prince." *Hmm... I guess he can be like that sometimes, but isn't he nice most of the time? In fact, he's not as self-centered as the game makes him out to be.*

Huh...? Game makes him out... to be? What am I even thinking about? It was like I'd met him in real life, as opposed to him just... being a character in a game...

"What's wrong?" Acchan asked, looking at me worriedly.

"Ah... it's nothing! Nothing at all. Oh, right! I have to eat!" Thanks to my form teacher's terrible lecture, I had lost half the time that I usually had for my lunch. I had to finish quickly... after all, my stomach was mostly empty. I'd only had an unseasoned cucumber for breakfast.

After I finished my lunch, which had been homemade by my mom, Acchan and I had a lot of fun enthusiastically talking about our otaku hobbies.

I woke up every morning, took Mom's homemade lunch to school, and happily spent time with my friends. That was my everyday life. It was a typical, unchanging routine. But for some reason… it felt nostalgic, somehow. Like a cherished memory.

Wouldn't it be great if I could keep living this way? For some reason, this thought floated into my mind.

A few days after that, I'd made good progress in *Fortune Lover*. In fact, I was now in the middle of a certain sadistic prince's route.

However… what was this feeling? Something about all it was… wrong. And the more I played *Fortune Lover,* the more I felt that way.

It was a mysterious feeling… as if I'd forgotten something that was very, very important to me. But no matter how much I thought about it, I couldn't quite figure out what exactly I was missing.

Those carefree days continued… until a certain lunch break. I was having my lunch with Acchan, like usual.

"How's your playthrough of *Fortune Lover* going?"

"Still on the route of the sadistic prince…"

For some reason, Acchan seemed a little worried when she heard my answer. And she seemed… different today. I couldn't put my finger on it, but she seemed more mature.

"How has school been? Fun?"

"…Huh? Hmm… yeah, I guess."

Yet another mysterious question from my friend. The more I responded, the more I felt like something about her was different. It was something about her face. I'd known her since middle school. We'd been together ever since then, but…

"Wha?!" I cried out in spite of myself. For a split second, Acchan looked different — I saw her as a beautiful young girl with stark-white hair and ruby-red eyes.

What am I even thinking? There's no way that could be what Acchan looks like. I rubbed my eyes and then looked at my friend again. And there she was, looking the same as always. *What did I just see, then? Was I just imagining things?*

A wide smile spread across Acchan's face as I continued staring at her, mouth agape and slightly frozen in place. "I'm having a lot of fun. After all, I got to meet you, and live through these days again. But... this isn't really your world anymore, is it?"

"Huh?" *This is no longer my world? What's she going on about?*

"You belong to another world now, don't you? Many people are waiting for you there."

"...Acchan? What... What do you mean?"

Acchan's answer to my confusion was a quiet, gentle smile. "Listen. Can you hear them? Calling out to you."

"Huh...?"

As if on cue, I found that I could suddenly hear a series of voices.

"Katarina... wake up! I cannot imagine a life without you."

"Wake up, please... Big Sister! Didn't you promise that we would be together forever?"

"Lady Katarina! Wake up, please wake up! If you aren't here... how can I keep going and working hard?"

"Hey, wake up! How long're you gonna keep sleeping, you idiot?!"

"Katarina... open your eyes. Please."

"I beg of you, Lady Katarina... please. Please open your eyes...!"

Those voices... sounded so nostalgic. I'd heard them before. It was as if a veil of mist was hanging over my mind. I couldn't remember what this was all about, but it felt wrong. And now, finally... that mist was lifting.

The familiar voices... of my brother and friends. All people who were important to me... How could I forget about them?

The mist faded away completely. Vivid memories flooded into my mind. Before I knew it, I had remembered everything.

It was as Acchan said. My noisy and naggy, yet loving family; my close friend and fellow otaku; the otome games I loved... They were all part of a calming, peaceful world. But it was a world I no longer belonged in.

After all, I had stepped into a different world a long time ago. I had formed bonds with important people there too — my new family, and my dear friends. And now... those important people were waiting for me.

I have to return to the world I belong to. The world where my important friends and family are all waiting for me. That thought resounded strongly through my mind.

With that, a sudden, mysterious sound rang through the air — it was the sound of something breaking.

Surprised, I turned to survey my surroundings. My classmates had all vanished without me noticing, leaving me with an empty classroom. The only ones who remained were Acchan and me.

The floor began to crumble before my eyes. We would soon be falling straight into what seemed to be a bright pool of light.

Ah... this is the place. If I keep falling... I'll return to the world I now rightfully belong to.

"Ah! Wait! There's one thing, Acchan! I have to save Maria when I return to my world! You must know where she's being held! Please tell me!" Acchan, after all, had cleared the game long before I did. If anyone knew, it would be her.

"Alright. Maria is still within the campus… in a hidden room on the grounds. The exact location is…" With that, Acchan concisely explained Maria's whereabouts.

The floor continued to crumble, the pieces falling into the light. There was no time. I should have figured it all out faster. Remembered quicker. I had so many questions to ask.

"Ah… one more thing. Why is the president…"

Why was there so much pain on his face? Why was he crying?

But my foothold was crumbling, and the light began to absorb me. Acchan looked at me with a serene expression.

"I'm sure you'll figure it out. Save the president… just as you have saved us. His real name is…"

"What?! Save? What do you mean? What real name?"

Unable to understand Acchan's words, I asked question after question. All the while, I could feel my body half-submerged, steadily sinking into the light.

I could no longer see Acchan's face. Somehow, I knew… that this would be goodbye. My precious friend, who had been with me for so long. It was all thanks to her that I even managed to get into high school in the first place. Acchan was always looking out for me.

But then… in that sudden accident, I was gone. I couldn't even say goodbye. This was my final chance.

"A… Acchan! It's been a long time… but I'm glad I could see you again! Goodbye, Acchan! Thank you for everything!"

Turning to Acchan, who I could no longer see, I shouted at the top of my lungs. Did my voice reach her…?

"I'm glad too, to have seen you again. This time… I will stay by your side, as Sophia. Goodbye and thank you, my dear, dear friend…"

Acchan's last words, however, did not reach my ears.

The first thing that I saw when I opened my eyes was Sophia's face, with large droplets of tears falling from her eyes. Behind her were Jeord, Keith, Mary, Alan, and Nicol. My treasured friends.

Ah… I have finally returned to my own world.

Sophia hugged me tight as I slowly awakened, before starting to sob loudly. Even the usually calm and collected Mary was hugging me too, tears flowing down her face.

Everyone else was looking at me with relief. I could tell just how worried everyone was. My world was right here, with all these important people. This was why I had to protect this world, and everyone in it.

A terrible Bad End like that… I refuse to let that happen!

The first thing I did upon waking was to stretch slowly. After all, I'd been fast asleep for the last few days. My body felt dull and heavy.

Although I immediately set out to look for Sirius Dieke, the student council president was nowhere to be found. Maybe he had heard of my awakening, and had escaped someplace… at least, that was what everyone else said. But I didn't think this was true.

I thought he must still be on the academy grounds, in that secret place where Maria was being held captive. When asked why I thought so, I couldn't answer. But I knew it in my heart — Sirius was currently with Maria, and she was safe, for now. That was why I had to go to that hidden chamber. I had to save Maria.

"He is a criminal who made an attempt on your life, Katarina. He is a dangerous individual. You should leave this to us and the authorities, and rest in your room."

So I was told. But… I wanted to save Maria with my own two hands. After all, I was the reason she had been captured in the first place. And also… I wanted to speak with Sirius one more time.

The image of his face, that expression of pain and suffering, was etched firmly into my mind. He had been crying without a sound. Even though he'd shown me such hostility, his expression looked sad enough to make me worry.

And then there was that last thing Acchan said… his true name. Sirius Dieke. There was something going on with him that went deeper than we knew. To understand what it was, I had to see him again myself. I had to make that journey.

Although they didn't want me to expose myself to danger at first, everyone eventually agreed, under the condition that I wouldn't go alone. And so we all set off together to find Maria and Sirius.

We found ourselves in a dark forest, some distance away from the academy's main buildings. Our target was a storage building that was closer to the Magical Ministry's laboratories than the student dorms, so it didn't see much traffic.

After pushing open the surprisingly heavy door, we entered cautiously into a space almost as big as the Claes Manor guest parlor. Various junk from who knows what was scattered all over the room. Avoiding the piles of clutter, we went deeper and deeper into the room.

I finally stopped, standing in front of a large shelf. We were now at the farthest point from the building's entrance. It was a heavy and imposing shelf — not one that a single person could move. But I quickly located a raised surface, like a button, that was hidden on the side. Exactly where Acchan said it would be.

I promptly gave the button a solid push. Almost immediately, the shelf slid over to one side, its movement almost completely silent. With the shelf now out of the way, we came face to face with what appeared to be a solid black door.

"It's really there…!" Everyone else exclaimed in surprise. I had told them earlier that I'd seen this whole hidden chamber in a premonition while I was asleep. While they looked at my doubtfully at first, they eventually believed me and followed me here. Though they still seemed hesitant, even now.

I reached out, placing a hand on the doorknob. I'd assumed that it wouldn't simply open, but I was mistaken, luckily. With a simple turn, the door swung open to reveal a small room about the size of my dorm room.

I stepped forward without hesitation. The room was lit only by a single, tiny window in the ceiling — it was a dark, dank space. After allowing my eyes to adjust, I looked around. It didn't take me long to discover the silhouette of a girl, sitting alone in a corner.

I immediately ran to her. "Maria!!"

"…Lady Katarina…?"

It was a painful sight. Maria had a shackle around one foot, connected to the wall by a thin chain. Thankfully, she didn't appear to be hurt. While she didn't exactly look like she was in the best of health, her eyes looked straight into mine, and her voice was steady.

"…Maria. I'm sorry I'm so late…" I held her tight. I had taken too long to come help her.

"…I should be the one to apologize… I have greatly inconvenienced everyone…"

Either because she was relieved or because she was exhausted, Maria's body began to relax in my arms.

"No, Maria! Didn't you do what you did for my sake?"

Maria nodded with a troubled expression. As I thought, she'd realized something and tried to help me by exposing the truth.

"Thank you, Maria."

A crimson flush crept into Maria's cheeks as she smiled faintly in response. I heaved a sigh of relief. But while it was wonderful that we'd found Maria unharmed, I still had one more goal left to achieve.

"Hey… Maria. He… Sirius Dieke is still here, isn't he?"

"…Yes, Lady Katarina. He is… just beyond that black door," Maria said, her expression darkening slightly as she pointed out the door in question. It was well hidden, to say the least. At a glance, it looked like a simple wall.

"…Do you already know what the president did to you, Lady Katarina?"

"Hmm… I guess I kind of so. But actually, there's still a lot I don't understand."

While I had discovered this hidden chamber thanks to Acchan's advice, there were still many unanswered questions. Why would the president do this? How did he even get his Dark Magic powers to begin with? Was he really capable of causing such a tragic and terrible Bad End, like he did in the game? So many questions, so few answers. Even so…

"…I still can't think of him as a bad person. That's why… I feel like I should at least speak with him, just one more time."

"Have you no sense of danger? Aren't you being too kind?" My friends around me protested, but even so… those were my honest feelings at that moment.

"Is that so…?" Maria said thoughtfully. "I suppose he hasn't done anything bad to me, other than placing this shackle around my leg. He brought me meals, too. Perhaps… he is not a bad person… But he does possess some mysterious powers, Lady Katarina…"

As Jeord thought, Maria, as a Wielder of Light, was able to detect the presence of the Dark Arts.

"...So you know about his powers?"

"Can you sense it too, Lady Katarina?"

"I've heard of it, but I can't sense it like you can. Only people with Light Magic can do that, right Maria?"

Maria nodded. "Yes... During the incident at the dining hall, there was some sort of black mist surrounding those girls, and the president too. In fact... the black aura around the president has only grown bigger and stronger in recent days..."

Huh?! Why? Did he use his Dark Magic on some unwitting victim again? When? What for?

Maria patiently continued her explanation. "But... that mist is different from what I saw before, Lady Katarina."

"...Different?"

"Yes... The mist I saw before was external. It almost... clung to him, like a film over his being. The mist now, however, seems to be coming out from within the president himself. If I had to describe it... it would almost seem like the mist is controlling him."

What does that mean? Did he lose control of his Dark Magic somehow, causing it to go berserk? I tilted my head this way and that, completely confused. Maria seemed equally at a loss, looking more worried by the second.

However... we had come this far. I wasn't going to simply give up and run away because it was "too dangerous" or some reason like that. My friends seemed to understand my feelings, so even though they didn't want to let me go, they didn't say anything to stop me. They knew that I was dead set on doing what I came to do, and wouldn't back down no matter what they said.

"...I'll come with you, Lady Katarina," Maria said, looking straight at me.

"But… you've been locked up in this place for all this time, Maria… you really should rest." Even if Maria hadn't been hurt, she was locked up in this small, dingy room for an extended period of time. She should get out of here as soon as possible and be examined by a doctor.

"No… I'm coming too! Am I not the only one who can perceive the president's mysterious powers, Lady Katarina?! Then it should be clear that I should come along too!"

Maria did have a point. She was the only one here who could perceive Dark Magic.

"Even if you say I can't… I'll still come along! Somehow!" Maria said, her courage reflected in her eyes. I could tell that she had already made up her mind.

We freed her, and soon we all found ourselves standing in front of the door, ready to enter.

This door, much like the previous one, opened without much difficulty. But this time we were greeted by a staircase instead of a room, extending deep underground. It was a narrow, unlit passageway. Only one person could fit through at a time. We all made our descent, with Jeord providing some lighting using his fire magic.

Before long, we discovered yet another door. Jeord, who was leading the group, placed his hand on the dark, heavy door, and pushed. It opened with hardly a sound.

For some reason, this room made me feel… sick. Although it was almost the same size as the chamber that Maria had been locked up in, there wasn't a single window through which sunlight could enter. By what little illumination the room had, we could make out some dark, sinister letters, lining the walls in an endless scrawl.

It felt like the air in this room had been frozen in time... and in the middle of it all was Sirius. Looking at his face, illuminated faintly by the lamp he held, I could tell that he was a lot worse for wear compared to the last time I saw him. When he turned to us, I could see just how exhausted he was. He looked like he'd given up. That is, until he turned his gaze to me.

"...Why are you here?" His expression immediately changed to one of shock.

Huh? I thought he already knew that I'd woken up, hid himself down here 'cause of that... did he not know?

"...Because the sleeping spell you cast on me was dispelled." Since Sirius seemed confused, I thought I should let him know.

"That isn't it! I KNOW that it was dispelled! Why would you appear before me, after what I did to you?!" Sirius exclaimed, his expression darkening.

"Oh, that. Right." My friends — all of them, actually — had said the same thing when I said I wanted to go to him. Now I was hearing the same thing from Sirius himself.

I suppose he does have a point. He did say some really mean things to me, and also used his Dark Magic to put me to sleep.

If I had continued to sleep, I definitely would have died... or at least, that was what everyone told me. In any case, I did manage to wake up, so the only real damage done here was my bones feeling a little stiff after having slept for two days straight. If anything, I probably needed that sleep — I felt a lot better now. And so I decided to answer Sirius truthfully.

"Well... I don't really think that you've done anything particularly terrible to me..."

"...You... Do you even know what was done to you?!"

Ah, that look. Sirius definitely thinks I'm a fool. Rude...

"No, I do know. You used your Dark Magic to cast a sleeping spell on me, right?"

"Exactly! And that sleeping spell would take your life!"

"Hmm... That's a lie, isn't it?"

"A... lie...?" Sirius' expression seemed to darken further. But I ignored it, continuing with my little speech.

"After all... if you really did want to kill me, you would have done it there and then, not simply put me to sleep. Isn't it faster that way?"

We had been alone in the courtyard. As far as I knew, there were no witnesses. It would have been easy for Sirius to kill me if he'd really wanted to. There was no point in going through the trouble of putting me to sleep.

While I wasn't exactly the sharpest knife in the drawer, even I could understand this. And Sirius was a really smart person; there was no way he wouldn't have realized what an opportunity he had. And so, I came to the conclusion that he never really intended to kill me in the first place.

"..." Sirius simply stared at me blankly, as if his words had been snatched away.

"I wanted to see you one more time, President. So we can have a talk."

"...Talk?"

"Yes. Because... you looked like you were in pain back then. Because you were... crying."

Honestly, I couldn't quite remember what I said back then. To be fair, I was put into a magically induced sleep for two days, so I can't be blamed for this lapse in memory. But I remembered one thing clearly from just before I collapsed: Sirius' tear-streaked face.

Why? Why did he have such a pained expression...? It was something that I couldn't stop wondering about.

"So... I wanted to see you one more time, to try to have a proper conversation..."

Sirius' face twisted in response. "...You conniving witch... And? Then what? Are you going to save me like you saved these other fools? Saint Katarina Claes?" His lips were twisted in loathing along with the rest of his face as he spat out his words.

Conniving? Save? Saint? I don't know what he's talking about.

Hmm... come to think of it, Acchan did say something about saving, didn't she? That I should "save the president"...

However...

"That's impossible!" I declared resolutely, keeping my gaze trained on Sirius. "I'm not the protagonist, after all! I am nothing more than a rival character, a villainess of a noble! There's no way I am capable of saving anyone!"

I guess there's no way Sirius could have predicted that response. His jaw dropped, and for a while, he was frozen in that baffled expression. I could hear my friends whispering too: "Rival character? Villainess noble?" Apparently they were also confused.

I had blurted out my answer before I could stop myself, despite the fact that no one would understand what I meant. They were probably all thinking about how strange I was. *"Ah, what peculiar things that girl says..."*

Even so, those words were the truth, and nothing but the truth. In the otome game world of *Fortune Lover*, I was not the protagonist, but the antagonist villainess rival character. That was my role. And I didn't even measure up to the other rivals, either — I couldn't hold a candle to Mary or Sophia, with their beauty, smarts, and magical strength.

I wasn't all that beautiful, I wasn't smart at all, and my magic was half-baked at best. *Yes, I'm the disappointing rival character. I am Katarina Claes. How could someone like me heal the trauma and pain of others, like the protagonist? Soothing someone's broken heart? There was no way I could do that!*

Even so, there was one thing I could do. Well, more like the only thing I could do.

"I can't save you from your pain... or make it go away. But... I can stay by your side."

I was, after all, nothing more than a villainess. I didn't have it in me to miraculously save other people. But... I could be there for them.

"I could stay with you. When you're sad, when things are hard... I can listen. I can stay until you're happy again, or maybe just okay again."

Suddenly recalling all the memories of my past life... realizing that I was a villainess... working so hard every day to achieve my goals. There were hard times and there were happy times.

And then there was everyone else. My dear friends who stayed by my side all this time. Who listened to me, who stayed with me until I could cheer up again. That was how I managed to come this far.

I was not alone. Standing beside me were my trusted comrades. Even if I alone couldn't hope to save Sirius from his suffering, or even make it fade... my friends would surely be able to offer him their help.

I slowly made my approach, taking a few steps towards Sirius. "So... you don't have to cry alone."

When I had seen his pained expression, his crying face... it was like a dam had broken inside him. What was hurting him so much? What was making him suffer? I knew nothing about what was going on. But... he'd been crying quietly, as quietly as he could, all by himself in a dark room. His pain was only getting worse and worse.

And then... when he reached his limit, perhaps we would all end up like that nightmare I had. That terrible Bad End. I couldn't let that tragedy come to pass!

"Come. Come with me... Raphael." I raised a hand, reaching out to the crying Sirius slowly. I called him by his name — his real name, that I had learned from Acchan.

Upon hearing those words, Sirius... no. Raphael's eyes opened wide. He stared straight at me. Honestly, I didn't understand what his real name meant. But somehow, it seemed like a more fitting name for him.

Raphael slowly raised his hand. Trembling, he reached it out towards mine. His skin was ice-cold. I raised my other hand, clasping it over his. "It'll be okay." I smiled, trying to cheer him up, even if only a little. And I focused on making sure my face didn't look like a grinning, wicked villainess who had something up her sleeve.

"...The black mist... it's fading..." Maria, who was standing some distance behind me, muttered. I didn't really know what she meant. But when I looked into Raphael's tear-filled eyes, I saw that they were a familiar, gentle color.

"What are you doing in a place like this?" said a soft voice from above my head.

I had been bullied by the other children who lived nearby, and had hidden in a corner of my home. Looking upwards at the direction of the voice, I saw my mother, whom I loved very much, looking down at me with worry.

"...It's nothing. I'm okay." I didn't want to worry my mother. I blurted my words as I rubbed away my tears in a hurry.

"If you cry in a place like this, all alone, those painful feelings won't go away. When it hurts, Mom will be by your side. I'll sit by you and listen to you, so don't cry alone," my mother said, holding me tight.

I had lived alone with my mother for as long as I could remember. She was always working hard while she raised me, but although it was hard on her, the smile never faded from her face.

We did not live comfortably, nor were we possessed of any means, but my mother always said the same thing: "I am truly blessed to have a wonderful son like you!" she would say, while hugging me tight. My mother loved me very much. Those were peaceful, blissful days.

I didn't know anything about my father. Not his name, not if he was dead or alive. Because of this, I was often picked on and bullied by the other children who lived nearby. It would be a lie if I said I didn't ever wonder about it, but my mother never spoke of my father. And, being a child, I didn't dwell on it too much.

However, I would eventually come to regret this. If I had at least known something about who my father was, then perhaps I would have been able to change what happened.

Eventually… the peaceful life I shared with my mother abruptly ended. It happened in the spring of my ninth birthday, in the evening, as my mother and I were walking home together.

Without warning, a few burly men I had never seen before ambushed us. They pressed a cloth to my face. It had a sweet smell to it… and that was the last thing I remembered.

When I regained consciousness, I found myself in a dark room.

The room didn't seem to have access to natural light, and was lit only by a lamp. By the light of that lamp, I could see sinister letters written all over the walls. It was so unsettling.

There were about a dozen people there. I was lying down on my back in the middle of the room, and those people stood, surrounding me.

The burly men who had restrained me before I passed out were also present. These must have been the people who brought us here.

My limbs were tied down. I tried to move, to no avail. There was also a cloth gag in my mouth — I was unable to speak, or make much of a sound at all.

Before me was a man dressed completely in black, and… a woman. The woman wore a vibrant red dress, and around her neck were several large jewels. She didn't seem to fit her surroundings very well.

"The child is awake. Quickly, now. Bring him here," the woman in red said, and one of the burly men stepped up. In his arms was what appeared to be a boy of my age. The boy was placed next to me, on top of a beautiful piece of fabric. It seemed like he was sleeping peacefully.

Now that I saw him up close, I saw that the boy was thin... very thin. He was also somewhat pale, and seemed to have trouble breathing. He seemed very ill indeed. However... looking past his afflictions, I noticed that he looked very similar to me. He had red eyes and grey hair. Even his face looked like mine. Who was this child...?

As I continued to inspect this boy, the woman in red started to speak. "With this, the preparations are complete. Let us begin. Present the sacrifice."

Preparations? What do they mean? Is something going to happen in this dark room? What do they mean by "sacrifice"? I felt like I had heard the word before, in a book my mother once read to me. *What was it, again?*

Still confused about the situation, I kept pondering the meaning of the word. Another man stepped forward — this one opposite the burly man who had placed the boy on the cloth. This man, too, seemed to be bringing someone along.

That person was... my beloved mother. He was dragging her into the room. Her beautiful face was bruised and battered. She was roughly pulled and made to walk, as if she had suffered injuries to her legs.

"Mother!" I yelled, desperately struggling against my cloth gag. In reality, only a slight, muffled sound escaped. I tried to get up, tried so hard to go to her. But one of the men standing near me pushed me down roughly, pinning me to the cold, hard floor.

"Stop it!" my mother shouted, trying to walk towards me. She, too, was subdued by one of the men.

Regarding us with a chilling stare, the red woman spoke once more. "Please do not be so rough with that child's body. After all, his body belongs to my precious Sirius."

That child? Does she mean me? What does she mean by my body belonging to this... Sirius? Who is Sirius? I couldn't understand what was going on at all.

"Madam Marchioness, please... if you hate me, do with me as you please... but please, please spare the child..." my injured mother pleaded with the red woman desperately. My mother referred to this red woman as "Madam Marchioness."

Does she know this woman? Why would she hate my mother? My mother was very kind to me. She was also very nice to everyone who lived around us. Everyone loved my gentle mother. I couldn't think of any reason why someone would hate her.

However, the red woman stared at my mother coldly. "What an impudent woman you are. First you take my husband from me, and then were gifted with a child... and yet you ask for more?"

"...I am nothing more than a passing fancy of the marquess, and was only with him for a short time. As I said before... I have no intention of approaching him ever again. All I want to do is live quietly with my child..."

A dry smack echoed across the room. My mother, who was pleading with the red woman, had been slapped across the face.

"MOTHER!" I tried to scream, but I was still gagged, unable to speak.

"...Both fathered by Marquess Dieke. Both children take after him... and yet. Why are we so different? Why are you so blessed with beauty and health? And yet I have nothing. I am not beautiful. I am sickly and unloved by my husband. When I finally bore my child, he was sickly too, and was born with an incurable disease. He has not long to live…" the red woman said, roughly grabbing my mother.

"…To think… That you two, mother and son, could live happily forever… I will not allow it! I will NEVER allow it! *Begin!*"

At her words, one of the men in black approached my mother, standing before her. In an almost emotionless voice, he started to speak. They were the most mysterious words I had ever heard; they sounded foreign, like the language of a faraway land. However, they were also strangely… familiar.

I could feel a wave of goosebumps rising over my skin as the man continued to speak. I felt sick. It was like the air itself stagnated and became still.

And then the man's words stopped. At that, the entire room was enveloped by a thick blanket of darkness. In the pitch-black dark, I couldn't see. All I heard was my mother's screams.

As soon as light began to enter my vision, I started searching for my mother. It didn't take long for me to find her. About two, perhaps three steps away, she was sprawled out on the floor. I desperately tried to go to her, struggling against my bindings.

Upon finally managing to get close to her, I noticed that my mother's face was pale. She was no longer breathing. Although she was injured before, she was not dazed like this. *Why? What happened?*

"*Mother! Mother!*" I yelled pointlessly into the gag. I saw myself reflected in my mother's eyes. She stared straight at me.

"…please…"

In a voice too faint to be heard, in a voice that sounded like it would fade away any moment… my mother took her last breath. And then all was silent.

"Well? Was it a success?"

"Yes. As stated in the texts… it would seem that the adequate powers have been attained," the man in black responded.

"Is that so? Then do it quickly. Use that power to transfer Sirius' consciousness into that child's body."

Although I could hear their conversation, nothing entered my mind. I couldn't accept what had happened here. Just moments ago, I was talking with my mother about what to have for dinner, and we were walking home together. Before I knew it, I had been taken to this dark place… and here, my beloved mother… stopped breathing.

"Yes. We shall begin." The man in black placed a hand on the body of the boy sleeping next to me, and then another on my head. In that moment, a rapid series of images filled my mind. They were strange images, complete with sound. Unknown places, unknown people… it felt like someone else's life.

As the images continued to flood my mind, I was assaulted by a searing headache. And then… as the images finally slowed down and stabilized, I found that I suddenly knew everything. Why I had been brought here, and why my mother had stopped breathing in this dark room. The images that entered my mind told me everything I needed to know. The plans of that woman in red…

The woman in red was the wife of Marquess Dieke, a noble. She was the mother of the boy lying down next to me. Sirius was his name. However, the Marquess did not love his wife. He was a womanizer, and continued sleeping around with other women even after he got married. The Marquess did the bare minimum for his wife. After ensuring that his heir was born, he quickly left, seeing no need to stay by his wife's side.

Perhaps that was the reason why the madam became intensely attached to her only son, Sirius. She would speak of her misfortunes to this young child every day. She became emotionally dependent on him.

However… the child, the one and only place where she could rest her heart, was soon afflicted with an incurable disease. She used all her money, all her power, and hired countless doctors. When those attempts failed, she even ventured into the occult. But no matter what she did, her son's health did not improve, and he got sicker with each passing day.

The woman could not accept that she might lose her only child. One day, she became aware of a certain kind of magic — Dark Magic. Magic that was able to dominate the hearts and minds of others. Magic that could replace memories. Upon hearing of that… an idea came into the woman's mind.

If she had transplanted her son's memories into a healthy body, he would surely be saved. It was a nonsensical plan. Realistically, such a reckless plan would have no hopes of success.

However… there was no other way to save her child. The woman, unable to bear the thought of losing her son, decided to chance it on this reckless plan. And so, the woman started to search for a way to obtain Dark Magic, and a suitable vessel for her son's memories.

The vessel, the new body for her son, had to be healthy. It also had to be of a similar age and appearance as her son. After all, a body that looked completely different could not claim to be the heir of the Dieke family. It was then that the woman found what she was searching for. A child about the same age as her son, with a similar appearance. It was almost like the boy had been born to serve as a vessel for Sirius.

That boy was the illegitimate love-child of Marquess Dieke and one of the maids in his service that he had laid his hands on. The maid worked at the Marquess' abode, and was well-loved by her employer. Soon after, a child was born to the maid, and it was around that time that she vanished from the household. Upon leaving the Marquess' service, she bore a healthy and happy child, a child that looked very much like the Marquess. After that, she lived happily with her son.

And so it was decided that this child would serve as Sirius' vessel. The woman successfully discovered a means to obtain Dark Magic: a human sacrifice. A living person had to be sacrificed to become a Wielder of Darkness. So the woman decided that she would sacrifice the former maid who was now so happily living with her child.

Finally, the woman carried out her plan. She captured the vessel-child and his mother, who was to be the sacrifice. She instructed one of her underlings with magical aptitude to sacrifice the child's mother. Once he gained Dark Magic, he would then use his powers to transfer Sirius' consciousness into that of the child.

As per the woman's plan, Sirius' memories would be transplanted into the vessel… me. Upon this happening, I would cease to exist, and would instead be reborn as Sirius Dieke.

However, even with all of Sirius' memories, all he had seen and heard, suddenly crammed into my head… I was still me. It was without a doubt that Sirius' memories were fresh in my mind, but that was all there was to it.

They were only memories — the boy called Sirius was nowhere to be seen. All I felt was a strong wave of sadness. *"I am tired. Please let me rest,"* it seemed to say.

Before Sirius had even become aware of himself, all he had to listen to were his mother's complaints and grudges. This carried on even as he fell into the clutches of an incurable illness. The boy had no choice but to listen, and now he only wished to be set free. Despite his age, this child was already tired of living. What flowed into me were only memories — Sirius' will was nowhere to be found.

As such, I never became Sirius. I only gained his knowledge, void of emotion. The woman's plan had failed. However, the new memories I had just acquired hinted at one important thing: If she realized this, she would have me killed on the spot.

I cannot die here. I cannot not die here... It was a strong feeling, stronger than anything I had felt up until then. *I cannot die. Not yet... not before fulfilling my mother's last wish...*

Before I knew it, the gag had been removed from my mouth. I suppressed my emotions as much as I could, and then turned to the woman I hated most in the world.

"...Mother dearest," I said, just as Sirius Dieke had referred to her.

Upon hearing those words, a wide smile came across the woman's face. "Ahh, Sirius! It is you! The Dark Magic succeeded!" she said, holding me tight.

I could feel myself shivering from the extreme feelings of revulsion and hatred. And yet I endured. I couldn't die here, not yet. I had to live... and fulfill my mother's last wish.

"...Well then, madam. My work here is done. Could I please return with my family to our homeland, now...?" the man in black asked, somewhat fearfully.

"Yes… you have done well. Thanks to you, my Sirius has finally obtained a healthy body."

"…Well then, can I please return to my family?"

"Oh, of course. I'll let you see them now. Men." The woman gestured to the men who had restrained me earlier, who had been standing in the corner of the room this entire time.

The man in black seemed to have a look of peace about him. The burly men approached him, and… pierced him with their swords.

"…Why…?" he asked, blood flowing freely from his body as he reached out with his hand.

"You said you wanted to return to where your family was, right? Well, your family is already in the afterworld… waiting for you." The woman smiled elegantly.

"…I only worked for you… because you promised me that you would… let me return to my family. After we… did all this… You… You lied to me…!"

"Did I really have a choice? After all… it is a taboo power. Few, if any, have obtained such powers before. But now that everything has come to an end… wouldn't it be dangerous to simply let you live, now that you are a Wielder of Darkness…?" The woman smiled, as if she were extolling a truth of the world.

The man in black, his face scrunched up in pain and fury, stared right at the woman. "…Curse you, curse you… I will never forgive you…! I will take away all of your… power, your social standing… no matter what… I will see that you fall into hell…" The man's outstretched hand brushed against one of my toes.

"What are you going on about? You are a dead man. Men, finish him." At her command, the men thrust their swords deep into their victim… and soon he stopped breathing.

At the same time, Sirius Dieke, the boy who had been lying on the cold floor next to me, breathed his last breath.

I lived my life as Sirius Dieke from then on. I swore to take revenge against the Dieke family — the people who had taken my mother's life and turned me into a tool.

It was soon after I had started living my life as Sirius Dieke that I noticed that I had strange, mysterious powers. I found that I was able to read the hearts of others, and to control their actions. This was Dark Magic. Honestly speaking, I didn't know why this power manifested in me in the first place. Even so, it was something I could use, and I welcomed its presence.

Since then, I lived only for the sake of revenge. Time passed by... and then I met her. The girl who said the same things my beloved mother did; the girl with the same gentle smile on her face, just like Mother's: Katarina Claes. Ever since I crossed paths with her, all I felt was a tumultuous vortex of emotions in my heart. My resolve to live for revenge... started to falter.

This was why I had to get rid of Katarina once and for all. I lulled her into a deep sleep with the Dark Arts. She would sleep forever, and eventually die.

However, my unbreakable spell was overcome. I understood this to be the case when I went to check up on Maria in her little hidden room, and saw that my Dark Magic had been undone. I should have been panicking over the situation, but instead, I felt a deep sense of peace.

The spell I had cast on Katarina was broken. With this, she would be saved. *Perhaps that is for the best,* I thought. With Katarina's awakening, my deeds would be brought to light. Surely I would be arrested and dealt with.

"You can't let yourself get caught here! You have to escape, so you may continue planning for your revenge!" the voice within me said forcefully. However... if I were caught here, then everything would end. Perhaps that was a good thing.

"Have you forgotten your mother's last words?" the voice said once more. I felt my heart stir.

"Please avenge me…" These were my mother's last words. I had lived all this time in hopes of fulfilling that dream. But I was… so tired. I no longer wanted to hurt anyone.

Once the authorities got wind of this, surely this place, with its hidden chambers known only to the Dieke family, would be discovered too. The chambers were originally constructed so that Madam Dieke could carry out occultic research in hopes of saving her son. Soon after, research in the chambers shifted to the Dark Arts. It was for these purposes that this place was built — hidden away in the forests, and yet still on the grounds of the Academy of Magic.

The place where my mother's life had been taken away. Where my life, my future, had been snatched from me. Perhaps it was fate for it all to end here. That was why I kept waiting in this hidden chamber. Waiting for my own destruction.

I did not have long to wait. Soon, I sensed several presences in the room I had locked Maria in. The chamber where I waited was set deeper into the ground. With the descending stairway and a thick door between me and them, I could not observe the situation in the other room.

However, the fact that I sensed a presence in that room was enough for me to understand. At last, Maria would be saved, and I would be arrested and detained.

"You can still escape! Quickly, use the Dark Arts on them! All of them!" the voice within me cried. The voice would not stop. And yet, I found myself quietly waiting for the end.

And so... after the sound of approaching footsteps down the stairwell, the door to my room opened. I had expected the authorities, perhaps armed with a variety of weapons. Instead, I froze upon recognizing a certain person in the group.

Jeord Stuart and Keith Claes were there. As they were student council members, I was not surprised to see them. The prince, who had long since lost his heart to Katarina, surely desired to arrest the one who had made an attempt on her life with his own hands. I had assumed as much.

But... no. I remained rooted in place, staring at the person before me. *Why is this person here?* I could not understand. I had said such hateful words, even made an attempt on her life. Then why... why would she appear before me now?

"...Why are you here?" I asked, only for her to answer almost absent-mindedly.

"...Because the sleeping spell you cast on me was dispelled." Katarina Claes stood before me, with the same attitude as always. It was almost like she'd forgotten what had happened in the courtyard... What I had done to her.

"That isn't it! I KNOW that it was dispelled! Why would you appear before me, after what I did to you?!"

"Oh, that. Right. Well... I don't really think that you've done anything particularly terrible to me..." Katarina said, as if nothing bad had happened at all.

I had set out to kill her. What was she thinking? Was she really that much of a fool...? Or did she really possess the forgiving, accepting heart of a saint? Or, perhaps... there was an even simpler explanation.

"...You... Do you even know what was done to you?!" I asked.

"No, I do know. You used your Dark Magic to cast a sleeping spell on me, right?" Katarina replied, as if it were the simplest, most obvious thing in the world.

"Exactly! And that sleeping spell would take your life!" I had no choice but to lay it out clearly, as Katarina seemed to have trouble understanding the scope of the situation.

"Hmm... That's a lie, isn't it?"

"A... lie...?"

"After all... if you really did want to kill me, you would have done it there and then, not simply put me to sleep. Isn't it faster that way?"

There it was again. That blatant, straightforward way she answered my questions. I found myself speechless.

She was right. It would have been much simpler for me to kill her, as opposed to going through the trouble of putting her to sleep. Then... why did I not just do that? No... I couldn't. I could not do it. In truth, I—

"I wanted to see you one more time, President. So we can have a talk."

"...Talk?" *What is this?*

"Yes. Because... you looked like you were in pain back then. Because you were... crying. So... I wanted to see you one more time, to try to have a proper conversation..."

Her aqua-blue eyes looked right into mine. I felt my chest tighten up. I could hardly breathe. The maelstrom of emotions ravaged my heart.

"...You conniving witch... And? Then what? Are you going to save me like you saved these other fools? Saint Katarina Claes?" I raged, feeling out of control. She knew nothing about me. Nothing. How could the daughter of a duke, raised happily and lovingly, ever understand?

Even if Katarina Claes had said something along the lines of how she would "save me," I would surely brush it off. No… I would despise her for being so full of herself — just the folly of some lovingly raised noble lady of a powerful family.

Unexpectedly, however… Katarina said the exact opposite.

"That's impossible!" she declared, staring straight at me. "I'm not the protagonist, after all! I am nothing more than a rival character, a villainess of a noble! There's no way I am capable of saving anyone!"

Protagonist? Rival…? I couldn't comprehend these words that she had uttered with such force. She declared that salvation was "impossible"…? I could not possibly hope to understand the thought processes of Katarina Claes. All I could do was stand, looking back at her with a blank expression. And then—

"I can't save you from your pain… or make it go away. But… I can stay by your side," Katarina said, smiling gently. "I could stay with you. When you're sad, when things are hard… I can listen. I can stay until you're happy again, or maybe just okay again."

It was just like what my mother had said to me so long ago. I had hidden in a corner and cried alone, not wanting to worry her. But when she found me, she held me tight, saying similar things to me. When I finally remembered that memory — I felt something break deep within me. It was like the fog in my mind had cleared.

In truth, I had always, always suspected, in a corner of my mind. *"Please avenge me"* was supposedly my mother's last words. But could my gentle, loving mother, who always worried more about me than herself, ever leave me with such words?

And now I remembered. I finally remembered that my mother had *not* left behind such hateful words. Why? How could I misremember in such a fashion?

My mother's actual last words were: *"...Please... live. Live on... be happy. I love you..."*

Yes. My mother had never sought revenge. Until the very end, up until her last breath... she had wished for my happiness. That was why I thought I should live on... that I *had* to live on.

Before I knew it, Katarina had moved close to me. "So... you don't have to cry alone." With a gentle smile, she reached out with her hand.

Why was my vision distorting? My cheeks were wet.

"Come. Come with me... Raphael."

Raphael. My real name. The name that my mother had given me. A truly important name. Slowly, I reached out with my hand towards Katarina's. But then...

"Hey. What do you think you're doing? Don't listen to the words of someone like that! In fact... they're careless, and have approached you. Take her hostage and escape! You can still escape!" the voice in my screamed, agitated.

I, however, turned to the voice and responded. *"I don't want to do anything like that. I've already had enough of revenge!"*

"...Wh-What?" The voice in me seemed afraid.

I asked it a question. *"Also... who are you?"*

I had lived my life according to the demands of this voice that preached endlessly about revenge. It was this very voice that had brought up the memory of my mother's last words. However... those last words were false. My mother never said such a thing.

It was this voice that had enticed me into doing all this. This "other me" who shouted about revenge, and who twisted my beloved mother's last words.

I finally realized it. This thing was not me.

My belief that this voice was me had clouded its true form. I could now see it for what it was. For so long, I thought that this voice was another side of me… In truth, he was the man in black. The very same man in black who had taken away my mother's life.

"*So… you notice at last.*" The man in black smiled bitterly in defeat.

"*…All this time. You've been controlling me… pretending to be me.*"

I remembered how his fingers had brushed against me right before his death. I supposed it was then that the Dark Arts had seeped into me and controlled my will. And that was how it twisted my mother's last words.

"*All I was doing was granting your wish. I was just helping you,*" the man in black said hatefully.

"*…Yes. I hated them… I hated them all. But I did not live on for the sake of revenge! I lived on so that I could one day be happy!*"

That was my mother's last wish — that I would live on, and find happiness. So… this man in black had to be erased. It was known that the Dark Arts could only be dispelled by the person who cast the spell… but this girl before me was proof that it could be overcome.

"It'll be okay." Katarina's warm hands gently held mine.

I stared at the man in black, focusing on a singular thought in my mind. "*…This is the end. There will be no more revenge. Your existence is no longer needed.*"

"Damn it all... who do you think was the one who had led you all this way? You are weak... you traitor..."

With those last words, the man in black vanished.

Looking up, I saw Katarina's gentle smile, and felt her warm gaze.

Sirius Dieke — real name Raphael Wolt.

He told us everything; about how he had been born to Marquess Dieke and a maid in his service, about how he was raised, and how he had been living as Sirius Dieke... and also about how he had obtained Dark Magic. Finally, he also told us about how he had been controlled for the past seven years by that very same Dark Magic.

Although everyone had planned on presenting him to the authorities and revealing him as the perpetrator behind this whole incident, their opinions changed once they heard Raphael's story. As for me, I had never considered prosecuting him for what he did.

Maria, too, decided to forgive him for confining her in that chamber. Apparently she had been looking at Raphael's eyes at the moment when the Dark Magic cast upon him was dispelled, and so she was convinced of the truth of his words.

However, Raphael decided that he should turn himself in to the authorities. "I want to tell them about all this myself. About my mother and I... and the man in black, and the real Sirius. Although I was being controlled, I still have a duty to speak of the things I have done..." Raphael declared.

And so, the sins of Madam Dieke, her men, and Raphael's own crimes were brought to light. A while after Raphael had turned himself in, news of Madam Dieke and her men being arrested spread across the circles of noble society. We never heard about what became of Raphael for his involvement in forbidden magic, nor was the incident ever made public. It was probably safe to assume that he was now atoning for his crimes somehow.

Amongst all the rumors flying around, there were no details about Raphael's fate. So I continued to worry, not knowing what had become of him.

Several months passed. We were now about a month away from the end of the school year. With the graduation ceremony occurring soon, the members of the student council were all busy. So, not wanting to get in the way, I decided to focus on my farm work. I set off for my dorm room, planning to retrieve my equipment.

"Lady Katarina Claes." A familiar voice was calling out to me.

I turned around. Standing there was an ordinary-looking, brown-haired young man who was wearing clothes that looked like the ones that Magical Ministry officials wore. He had an unremarkable, almost boring appearance. If he hadn't said anything, I probably would have walked past him without noticing he was there. He didn't stand out at all.

Hmm? Who's this? The fact that he had called out to me and knew my name meant that I must know him somehow... but I couldn't remember him.

As those thoughts crossed my mind, I looked into the boy's eyes. It was then that I realized that those were the gentle grey eyes I knew so well.

"...Wait... could it be? Raphael?" I blurted out.

As I did so, Raphael's eyes opened wide. "I am surprised you could tell. Especially since my appearance has changed so much."

Wow, it is him after all... I hadn't seen him for a few months, and he did look completely different. But those gentle grey eyes were the same as always.

He smiled, as if embarrassed, when I explained how I'd known. It was a smile I hadn't seen in a long time.

"You've come back?" I asked. The fact that Raphael was standing here meant that he was able to return to the academy... or so I assumed.

"Yes. Thanks to the various testimonies that everyone provided, I was able to return here once more."

We all did what we could to help Raphael's case. We told the authorities what we knew of his story, provided Maria's eyewitness testimony, and explained how he had been gentle and kind to us up until then. We also used our social connections to send a petition to the highest levels of authority in the land. If any of that helped him, even a little, then it was all worth it.

I was really surprised by his new appearance. It was so different than it was before. Why did he change how he looked so much? "Could it be that... you're thinking of attending the academy again, as a new student...?" I asked.

After the incident, Raphael had left the academy. The official story was that he had left to recover after having some health issues. But since rumors of Madam Dieke's arrest had already spread through noble society, a lot of people assumed that her son, Sirius, was also involved.

It would be difficult for Raphael to enroll as Sirius Dieke again, especially with that face, which was widely known to the student body. However... now that he had changed the way he looked so much, it might be possible for him to attend the academy again as someone else. That was the thought that came to mind as I inspected Raphael's new appearance.

"No, I will no longer return to the academy. It is unfortunate that I could not graduate. However, I have actually obtained a position at the Magical Ministry, and will be working there from here on out. As Raphael Wolt, of course."

Once the Dark Magic that had been cast on Raphael dissipated, the source of his power went with it. He could no longer use the Dark Arts. Even so, he had high magical aptitude, and was apparently offered a position within the Ministry.

There was another angle to this, though. Considering that Raphael had been acting under the influence of forbidden magic for so long, it made sense that they would want to keep an eye on him. In other words, he was now under the Ministry's supervision and care.

Due to these circumstances, Raphael was assigned to work at the research facility on the academy's grounds. That was why he had to change how he looked — to make sure he wouldn't be recognized by the student body and cause a commotion. As for how he managed to look like a totally different person, apparently he had the assistance of a professional disguise and make-up artist.

A professional... disguise artist? What sort of profession is that? They even changed his face shape... It really does look like a professional's work. Apparently, he would need to stay in this disguise until noble society calmed down and forgot about the incident.

219

"So then, I guess that means we'll see each other again sometime?"

"Yes. I would think so... we are on academy grounds, after all."

"Heheh. Then, if you have the chance, can you make me your special delicious tea?"

"Of course. Gladly." Smiling, Raphael suddenly knelt before me, reaching out with his hand. It reminded me of when Jeord had proposed to me.

Huh? What? What's this all about? What should I do?

"Lady Katarina Claes... allow me to introduce myself once more. I, Raphael Wolt, would like to stay by your side. Would you permit me the honor of doing so...?"

Hmm... He's being so formal. I guess he means that... he wants to be friends from now on?

"Of course. Let's be friends," I said, holding his outstretched hand in mine. "Oh, but it's weird to hear you be so formal. Let's just go back to the way things were, hm?"

In response, Raphael smiled hesitantly as if he were at a loss for words.

Finally, the time had come. It was now the night before our second-year seniors would graduate. Alone in my dorm room, I balled my hand into a fist.

I had finally reached this point. The end of *Fortune Lover*, the last event… the graduation ceremony at the Academy of Magic.

A year would have passed since the commoner protagonist, intermingling with her noble peers, began attending the Academy of Magic. She would have furthered her studies, fallen in love with someone her age or a senior in the student council, and with the graduation of her second-year seniors, the game would end.

At the ceremony, the protagonist and love interest character would finally establish a meaningful connection. Though there was also a reverse harem route where she ends up with all the romanceable options.

Though I had safely overcome the Public Prosecution of Katarina Claes, I still had to be careful. I couldn't let my guard down until the game ended. Honestly, though… I couldn't imagine being chased out or cut down by any of these people. After all, they were now my close friends. But even so, I had to stay vigilant until the end.

I was armed with my greatest work — the toy snake that Grandpa Tom and I had designed and perfected — in my pocket. And if I were ever exiled from the kingdom, I would be ready. I had already prepared my farming overalls, my favorite hoe, books on agriculture, and various other tools. And I'd even become known for my skill with the sword lately.

I had the perfected ultimate projectile snake and the technique to quickly launch it. With the guidance of Mary and her green thumb, the crops I grew no longer wilted, and instead thrived. And day after day, without fail, I toiled away at the fields to hone my skill with the hoe.

Since my memories of my previous life came back to me on that fateful day, eight years ago, I have worked hard. Now, it is finally time to put my skills to the test.

If you're coming for me... then show me what you've got, Catastrophic Bad Ends! I, Katarina Claes, with her eight years of hard work, will be your opponent! I raised my balled fist to the air.

As I let my fighting spirit run wild, I was interrupted by a knock on the door. Then, Anne soon entered the room.

"Young miss, I do recall you saying that you wished to personally prepare the flower bouquet for Master Nicol. It is to be handed to him tomorrow to congratulate him on his graduation. Have you made the necessary preparations?" Anne said, eyeing me suspiciously as I kept my fist raised in the air.

In this particular academy, there was a custom where an underclassman would give a gift to a graduating senior, usually one who has acted as a mentor to them. It wasn't too different from what we did at my school in my previous life. I planned to get a gift for Nicol and hand it to him myself. After all, he'd been helpful to me in all kinds of ways.

Traditionally, these celebratory gifts were flower bouquets. There were sometimes bouquets with valuable accessories in them, or in some cases items with actual money. But gifts like that were usually only given if the two shared a particularly special bond.

I'd thought to myself that all I'd have to do is arrange a simple bouquet of flowers. But then I'd realized: Nicol, the Alluring Count, was really popular. In fact, his fanclub called "The Devotees" was probably the largest in the academy. He would receive countless bouquets.

So… I felt like he probably didn't need anymore. And anyway, getting bouquets meant that you'd have to put in the extra effort to preserve the flowers, and they weren't useful beyond being decorative. So I planned to give him something special instead.

With that in mind, I proudly showed Anne what I'd prepared. At a first glance, the item appeared to be a beautifully wrapped bouquet. But when you looked closer, you'd realize that it was completely different.

"Well? Ingenious, right?"

"…"

Ah, such a great idea! I really am a total genius!

The preparations for Nicol's congratulatory gift are complete! The Catastrophic Bad End countermeasures are in place!

"…Um. Young miss… what exactly is…"

Tomorrow is the day! The final battle!

"…Excuse me… young miss? Are you listening?"

I lifted my fist high once again, raising it triumphantly to the ceiling.

And so, I ended up staying up very late on the night before the final battle.

The graduation ceremony was similar to the opening ceremony I'd attended earlier in the year. The representative of the graduating students was Nicol. Originally that role belonged to Sirius Dieke, but he wasn't an option anymore since he was gone from the academy.

Regardless of gender, I found that a majority of people in the crowd had turned red and were sighing in a bittersweet fashion during Nicol's graduation address. They had all been thoroughly charmed by the Alluring Count. What a terrifying power...

Jeord, meanwhile, was the representative for the first-year students. He would become the student council president next year. I saw a similar reaction from the female students as the prince gave his speech; their faces were red, and a cacophony of sighs broke out. As expected of the fairy-tale prince.

With that, the student addresses peacefully concluded amongst the sighs of the crowd.

At least, the time had come. To me, this was it — the final boss. The ending event of *Fortune Lover* was finally under way.

It was time for the graduation party. With the ceremony over, almost all the students moved to an area with a standing buffet in the academy's courtyard. During this party, the protagonist and her love interest would sneak out of the venue quietly... and finally confess their passionate feelings for one another, forming an everlasting connection.

I decided to closely observe Maria's movements so that I could figure out who she would sneak out of the venue with. With that goal in mind, I stuck even closer to her than I normally would.

But I couldn't simply stay close to Maria and do nothing else — after all, this was a graduation party. I had to say a few congratulations to my seniors, at the very least. Of course, the senior I wanted to congratulate the most was Nicol, and I had to hand him his bouquet.

Maria and I made our way over to where he stood. By the time we got there, Nicol was already holding a sizable number of bouquets. In fact, there was also a small stand set up next to him where a pile of other bouquets now lay.

There were even more than I expected. The sheer number of them was stunning. Apparently many people wanted to congratulate him.

Maria was first to hand over her flowers. Although the bouquet that she had prepared was by no means expensive, it was charming and sweet, a very good reflection of her taste.

I stepped up next, handing Nicol the special bouquet I had prepared. Taking a glance at what appeared to be flowers, he smiled — that rare, wonderful smile of his. But once he took a closer look at the bouquet, he suddenly froze.

Noticing Nicol's strange behavior, Alan, who'd been standing next to him all this time, leaned over for a closer look. "Hey, what's wrong… pfft! What?! WHAT IS THIS? GRASS?!" Alan exclaimed, and soon his loud voice drew the attention of Jeord and Keith.

"Rude!" I responded to Alan tersely. "Grass? How could that be? They're vegetables!"

"…Vegetables?" Alan repeated, shocked. He leaned over again to give the bouquet a closer look.

Nicol, too, started inspecting the bouquet he held in his hands. Jeord and Keith remained standing off to the side, observing from a distance.

"I thought you might be troubled by all the bouquets you would get, so I wrapped up some vegetables from my field instead. It won't be just some decoration you throw away! You can eat them, too, and they'll fill your stomach!"

Not a flower bouquet, no! I name this invention the "veggie bouquet"!

My fields didn't have many leafy greens this time of year, so the center of the bouquet was mainly comprised of onions, chives, garlic, and things like that. Maybe it was a little grass-like, but unlike grass, these crops could be eaten!

What a great idea of mine! At least, I thought so, and I was full of praise for myself. Unfortunately…

"…Yeah no, it's definitely grass. Veggies? Seriously…? Pfff…" For some reason, Alan lost it and started laughing his head off.

What's so funny? How rude, Alan.

Nicol, finally having snapped out of his frozen trance, managed to respond at last. "Thank you. I shall… treasure. This meal."

Maria seemed to have high praise for the bouquet too. "It does look very delicious."

Meanwhile, Jeord was once again staring at the ground, his shoulders shaking. Keith, on the other hand, gave me his usual exasperated stare.

Before I knew it, the party moved on to its final phase. Honestly, I was totally panicked and nervous at this point, because Maria hadn't shown any signs of trying to leave the venue at all.

Even stranger was the performance that was being held as a surprise event for the seniors. *…A violin duet with Jeord and Alan? What? Don't you two care about sneaking out with Maria? What's this happy performance all about?* It was amazing that the day had come where those two would get along well enough to perform with each other. *Hmm. Was there even a scene like that in the game?*

227

I was also confused by how the two of them had asked me what songs I liked to listen to before the ceremony. *I didn't understand why they were asking, but... isn't this the song I just randomly chose? Why would I, of all people, who has nothing to do with the ceremony, be asked to choose the song selection?*

Hmm... The more I thought about it, the more confused I got. There were too many differences from the original scenario of Fortune Lover. *Maria was no exception, even saying "I truly am happy to be able to spend the whole day with Lady Katarina..."*

Well... I guess it's good that she's happy. But... Maria! Don't you have a romantic interest in mind?

Oh! Or perhaps... she's gone for the reverse harem route, and has already formed connections with everyone else here!

I never personally cleared the reverse harem route, and so I don't know anything about that particular ending. But if what Acchan said is true, I think Katarina does meet a Catastrophic Bad End in this one too...

Ugh, what is it going to be?! Is it really a reverse harem, Maria? Or are you going to choose someone?!

Panic, panic, panic... I couldn't restrain myself. I couldn't wait any longer.

"Hey... Maria. Do you have anyone you like?" A straightforward question was the way to go.

Maria seemed extremely surprised by my question, her face soon turning bright red. "I... really admire *you*, Lady Katarina..." she said in the most innocent way.

"...Um, Maria. While I am very glad that you think so highly of me... I don't mean that. I'm talking about... you know. Someone who has caught your fancy, a man who you want to date, right? That's what I meant." I made sure to be painstakingly clear with my question this time.

"…Caught my fancy… a man… who I would like to date…" Maria mumbled the words under her breath, as if giving them deep thought. I stood by her faithfully, holding my breath as I watched over her.

Quickly, now! Tell me, Maria! Which of these potential love interests is it?

"…I don't think there is anyone like that, Lady Katarina."

"…Wha…?" Maria's answer caught me off-guard, and a pathetic sound arose from the depths of my throat. *Huh? What? Did she just say that… there isn't anyone like that?*

Maria, however, continued confidently in spite of my confusion. "There are no men who have caught my fancy, Lady Katarina. But… someone did. She is someone I deeply admire. Someone whom I would like to be with forever — *you*, Lady Katarina." Maria grasped both my hands in hers. "So… please, Lady Katarina. Let me stay with you… for now and always."

Those are words that I've heard somewhere before… hmm. Oh, right. Those are the protagonist's final words to the successfully romanced love interest character. "Let me stay with you… for now and always."

But then… why me? I don't get it. I don't understand. Panic!

Suddenly, another hand approached ours. "Lady Maria… it simply won't do, leaving us out like that. I, too, would like to remain with Lady Katarina forever."

Saying so, I found my hands taken from Maria's grasp and into Mary's. Mary was smiling elegantly.

"M-Me too! Me too, Lady Katarina! I want to be with you… forever!" Sophia said, visibly excited, as she stood next to Mary.

"Well… then. I, as well. As much as I would be permitted to." Nicol chimed in too, with his usually stoic expression.

Before I knew it, Alan, who had apparently finished his duet at some point, showed up as well. "Th-Then! Me too, yeah?"

"Ah, everyone. What are you saying? Katarina is my fiancée, after all." Saying so, Jeord snatched my hands out of Mary's… only for them to be intercepted by yet another pair of mysterious hands in the process.

"Prince Jeord. I believe we have discussed this countless times prior, but my sister is hardly cut out for the role of queen. Please do cancel the engagement. I will take all responsibility for the needs and wants of my sister," Keith said, now holding my hands in his.

With that, my surroundings were suddenly enveloped in a hurricane of voices.

"Ah, Keith. How many times have I said it, hmm? I have no intention of canceling the engagement. Katarina will become my queen."

"But I must protest, Prince Jeord. It is unthinkable that you would have my important sister all to yourself. I will see to it that the engagement is canceled."

"It is as he says, Prince Jeord. Having Lady Katarina all to yourself? Unthinkable! We will ensure that the engagement is called off. To that end, I, Mary Hunt, shall lend you my strength, Master Keith."

"Yes… that's right," Sophia piped up. "I wouldn't want Prince Jeord… to have Lady Katarina all to himself. Please let me help too, Lady Mary… Oh, you should help too, Big Brother."

"If that is what you desire."

"Huh? Then I'll help too!" Alan jumped in.

"I will be of assistance as well! Please, do allow me to assist!" Maria spoke up passionately.

"Ah… how terrible, to gang up on me like that. Listen, all of you… I will never hand Katarina over."

Before I knew it, my hands, which had been in Keith's grasp moments ago, were free. But... it was happening again. I was being excluded from the conversation. I didn't understand what anyone was talking about anymore. It was lonely... but their discussion was lively, and everyone seemed like they were having fun.

My friends were all getting along... but this was not love. If it were the reverse harem scenario, things would feel different than this. Come to think of it, the atmosphere changed when Mary and Sophia joined us. While it did feel like I was being left out, it didn't seem at all like I was coming near a Catastrophic Bad End.

Still confused by recent events, I racked my brain, thinking as hard as I could. *Hmm... This... This situation. If I had to put it into words... an ending where everyone became friends? The "Friends Ending"?*

The "Friends Ending"... commonly known as the normal end. The protagonist does not end up forming a lasting romantic connection with a potential love interest, and the game ends with everyone simply being good friends. For a game about romance, to get an ending in which the protagonist falls in love with no one was a bad ending in some ways.

I didn't know why Maria said those specific words usually reserved for a love interest... and there were many differences with the friendship ending that I had seen in my previous life. Even so, from the happy look on all their faces, it did seem like the "Friends Ending" that I experienced before.

Honestly... I was sure that all the potential love interests would be smitten with Maria. After all, she was sweet and lovely. Even the heart of a rival character like me skipped a beat when I saw her face — that cute, shy look with crimson-tinted cheeks...

231

And then there was Keith and Jeord, who would often pull me away from Maria whenever we got too close. I'd assumed that they were already charmed by her, and were jealous of the time we spent together.

This was why I thought that Maria had already formed a connection with someone — if not everyone. And yet... here we were, at the Friends Ending instead.

Rival characters didn't have any ill fates befall them at the end of this ending. In other words, I, Katarina Claes, would not have to face a Catastrophic Bad End. I could feel the tension fade from my shoulders — it was as if all the strength in my body had evaporated.

Now fully relaxed, I looked at my friends, who were still having their lively conversation. Before long, we were told that the party had officially ended. And that was that.

And so it came to be that the graduation party, as well as the events of *Fortune Lover*, came to an uneventful end.

It was an unexpected ending — one that I hadn't imagined at all. To me, though... it was the best ending I could ask for.

With the graduation party finally over, we made our way to the student council chambers to hold a private farewell party for Nicol. While it seemed excessive to have one party after the next, this little gathering would just be having tea and snacks casually while hanging out.

We also invited the former student council president, Raphael, to the farewell party. We had to be stealthy, though, so that the students on campus wouldn't find out. When he arrived, he was somewhat withdrawn at first, but everyone welcomed him warmly. Since we were his juniors we had a flower bouquet for him too, which he graciously accepted.

However, he did freeze up a little at receiving my specially crafted veggie bouquet, just like Nicol did. Stunned by the sight of my amazing invention, I'm sure.

The student council was together for the first time in what seemed like forever. I had a lot of fun spending time with everyone.

"Here, Lady Katarina," Raphael said with a smile as he offered me a cup of tea.

"Thank you very much." After gratefully accepting the cup, I raised it to my lips with excitement. While it had been quite a while since I'd had the chance to enjoy one of Raphael's brews, its taste remained unchanged. It was as gentle as ever.

From what I was told, Raphael had been practicing tea-brewing for a long time, apparently always preparing a cup for his tired mother when she returned home from work. He had a calm and peaceful expression on his face as he recounted this to me.

"Lady Katarina... please do try some, if you would like..." Maria said, offering me some baked treats.

"Wow! These are exceptionally delicious! I've never seen treats quite like these before, Maria. Are these homemade too?"

They were soft, fluffy sponge cakes drizzled with dollops of syrup. Just looking at them was enough for me to start drooling. I had never seen her bake something like this before.

"Yes. A new concept, Lady Katarina. Mother and I thought of it together."

"Oh! With your mother?"

"Yes. I was happily telling her about how you enjoyed my treats, Lady Katarina, when she asked if you would be bored by having the same kind over and over again... so we thought of a new recipe together."

"Really? Ah, but I'll never get tired of your homemade treats, Maria! Never! But yes, I am very happy! Thank you very much for thinking of me. Please pass my thanks along to your mother for me."

"Yes. I will make sure to do so," Maria replied, smiling happily.

Having tried one, I quickly came to the conclusion that Maria's new cake was even more delicious than it looked. I could hardly stop my hands from moving.

"Katarina... if you eat so much all of a sudden, won't you have yet another stomach ache?"

"Exactly, Big Sister. You also had quite a lot to eat... more than most others, I would say, at the graduation party. Do limit yourself..."

So came the swift warnings from Jeord and Keith, as I continued stuffing my face full of snacks. *Ugh... they're both staring at me... Just like Mother does... I suppose they would be annoyed if I got a stomach ache from overeating...*

Jeord's deliberate warnings were delivered with a smiling face, while Keith simply looked worried as he continuously reminded me to eat less. *I guess I have no choice. I'll save some for later.* I slowed my snacking speed down — just by a tiny bit.

"Lady Katarina... I purchased a new series of novels recently. It turned out to be a most enjoyable story... if you would like, we could read it together next time," Sophia said.

She described the new romance series she had read. It was a story that sounded really interesting to me, so I decided to borrow the books right away. *Yes! I can't wait to read this.* With that, the conversation shifted to romance novels.

"Katarina. I fear I shall not see you for quite some time. I leave my sister in your care," Nicol said with his usual stoic expression.

"Ah, of course! We'll have a great time together," I replied with my best smile. And... there it was! Nicol's alluring smile flitted across his features for a moment.

...Nicol's alluring charm is fearsome indeed... even for someone like me, who's known him across the years and has built up some resistance to it. My cheeks were already red in spite of myself.

I wouldn't be able to see Nicol often after he left — at least, not for the next year. It would be a little lonely for me, but I suspected it would be much worse for Sophia, who loved her brother very much.

"Big Brother, do visit often! We have to ensure that you do not fall behind, given that you will be left out of the competition for a year!" Sophia pleaded, apparently hoping that Nicol would visit the academy when he could. I didn't really understand what the second half of her statement meant, though. In any case, Sophia really did love her brother.

"Ah, Lady Katarina. Have you already decided what crops to plant next year?"

I was still staring at Sophia, her face full of love and smiles for her dear brother, when Mary asked me that question. *Hmm... Mary does have a point. It'll be spring soon. What should I plant this year...? New vegetables of some kind, maybe? Hmm.* It was worth looking forward to.

"I would be glad to assist you this year too, Lady Katarina," Mary said. With the assistance of Mary and her green thumb, I felt like I had the farming capabilities of a thousand men.

"Fields, huh... I guess that's fine, but that thing you wear when you do fieldwork... Can't you wear something else? It makes you look like some kind of weird old commoner lady," Alan lamented.

I'd heard this complaint from him many times before. Honestly, I really liked my overalls. They were easy to move in, and they were perfect for field work. But if he was going to be that way about it, I supposed I should make some changes.

"...Fine, okay. I'll make some alterations." It was true that the overalls and headscarves that I'd been wearing were really plain, with boring colors. I guess it was inevitable that wearing them would make me look like an old lady. *Well, I'll try to include some patterned fabrics in my headscarves in the future!*

With my stomach now plenty full, I stepped away from the table and went to a nearby windowsill. Maybe standing would help with my digestion. Everyone was having fun talking about all kinds of things, seemingly relaxed and happy. But I couldn't help but think about the events of the past eight years.

Eight years ago, on the day that I turned eight... the memories of my past life came flooding back to me. It was then that I knew that this was the world of *Fortune Lover*, and that I had somehow been reincarnated as a villainess rival character who had nothing but Bad Endings in her future. When I'd realized all that, I'd thought to myself that this was a terrible thing to happen.

But now that I'd actually lived through the experience, I discovered that things were completely different from how they were in the game. Jeord, who didn't care in the slightest about Katarina, was now so close to me. Keith, who originally spent most of his life avoiding his adoptive sister, was now always looking out for me. Even those who the original Katarina was never destined to meet — Mary, Alan, Sophia, Nicol, and Raphael... they were now all my dear friends.

In fact, even Maria, the protagonist of the game, who was supposedly Katarina's arch-rival and the one responsible for many of her Bad Ends… was now an important friend of mine.

"Lady Katarina, are you alright…?" Maria asked, seemingly worried at the sight of me absentmindedly rubbing my belly as I stood next to the window.

"I'm fine, Maria. Thanks for asking."

Back then, I often said to myself… *How awful! Being reincarnated as Katarina Claes, the villainess! I really have nothing going for me!* But in the end, not a single one of those Catastrophic Bad Ends ever came to pass. Instead, I now found myself surrounded by many friends who cared for me, looked out for me, and offered me their assistance. I had truly made some wonderful friends.

While I didn't have much in the way of magical capabilities, nor was I good at my studies, my friends never once left my side. They were always there, offering me their support, even when it was painful or difficult.

Now, I felt like I could say it proudly, and as loudly as I could. To be able to cross paths with so many wonderful people… I was truly blessed.

The sun's warm rays caressed my cheeks, shining through the window… as if heralding the imminent arrival of spring. With this, a new season would sweep across the lands — a new season… beyond the plot and scenarios of *Fortune Lover.*

The End

It has been a year since we began attending the Academy of Magic. We are now second-year students and I, Jeord Stuart, have been appointed student council president.

The academy's systems, much resembling a meritocracy, ensure that only the capable would serve in the council. The position of president, of course, is also determined by academic achievement. As such, it is perhaps natural that one such as myself would be chosen for the role — after all, the position of top student belonged to none other than me.

In the past, I would have simply seen all this as an inconvenience, and would not even have taken tests seriously. Now however… Well. An inconvenience still, but a hoop I obediently jumped though. All for the position of student council president.

The purpose of this is simple — to make known far and wide the capability and skill of Jeord Stuart. With my social standing established, I will be able to ensure with certainty that the one I desire shall fall into my hands. In the past, I saw the seat of king as a burden, and never once even dreamed of taking on such a troublesome role. Now, however… If it is required so that I will be able to take her hand, I will gladly obtain such a position.

There was one more point. In showing my capability, skill, social influence and position, I will be able to ensure that a certain individual remains protected. Being the natural charmer that she is, she has many allies. Yet she is seemingly incapable of understanding the concept of danger. She is defenseless. One would question if she is truly the daughter of a noble — exasperating. To make things worse… she never thinks to suspect the motives of another.

The possibility of her being manipulated by some black-hearted noble, should I take my eyes off her, is far too high. As such, it is imperative that I solidify my social standing. My gaze from the sidelines will serve as a suitable warning to all those who would dare think of harming her.

With those reasons in mind, I will continue carrying out the troublesome role of student council president — all for the sake of solidifying my social standing.

After the lessons for today ended, I found myself in the student council chambers, where I carried out my duties.

"My work for today is done. If you would excuse me," I said, standing up from my seat.

If this had been a busy period, I would have been obligated to assist the others. There were no problems, however, given that we were not in a particularly busy season.

"You are already done, Prince Jeord…?" Maria Campbell asked, her voice full of surprise. She, too, had been appointed to a new position this year — that of vice-president.

"Yes. I will be returning to my quarters. Do excuse me."

Although my workload as the president was significantly heavier than that of the other members, it was nothing to me should I put my mind to it. Under normal circumstances, I would finish my work at the same time as the other council members. Today, however, I finished early, having diligently finished my assigned tasks.

After all, *she* was absent from the council chambers today. If she was not here, then there was only one place she could be, logically speaking. With me finishing my work early and heading off to see her, I could have her all to myself — if only for a short while.

As if deducing my intent, Keith Claes, another member of the student council, shot me an intense gaze. Mary Hunt, too, looked around this way and that stealthily, visibly quickening the movements of her pen.

Although the two would surely catch up eventually, it seemed that there was still some time. I headed out of the student council chambers, quickening my pace so I could have as much time with her as possible.

Leaving the council chambers behind, I walked beyond the bounds of the campus' academic buildings, heading for a certain corner of the academy grounds.

As I thought, that was where she was: Katarina Claes, dressed up as a commoner and happily working the fields. Katarina, my fiancée, had seen it fit to turn a small corner of the campus grounds into a crop plot.

The one person whom I desired to fall into these hands of mine. "Katarina."

Katarina turned around, looking surprised. She had not noticed me, it seemed. "Oh, Prince Jeord… is your work at the council already done?"

"Yes. Are you planting seedlings today, Katarina?" I asked, upon noticing what appeared to be rows of vegetable seedlings lined up neatly in a corner of the field.

"Yes. They just arrived yesterday, and so I thought I should plant them as soon as possible!" Katarina replied with a happy smile on her face.

This was how my fiancée was; she seemed to be happy anywhere she went, whatever it was that she did. There was not a single moment of boredom in my time spent with Katarina. The days I spent with her were filled with radiant light.

It made me wonder, however. *When was it that I first saw Katarina as a beautiful and radiant individual...?* Before I knew it, the young girl known as Katarina Claes... had become the most important thing in my life.

I approached Katarina, who was still joyfully explaining the intricacies of seedlings — and then, I placed a single hand upon her soft cheek.

"Hmm...? Prince Jeord?" she said, curiously, looking up at me with her azure eyes. To think that I could be this elated simply because I was the only thing reflected in her eyes...

"There was some dirt on your cheek, you see."

"Ah, is that so? Thank you very much." Katarina thanked me in her usual straightforward way. How defenseless. It was as if suspicion itself remained an unknown concept in her mind.

Usually, someone would get in my way right around this point. Those interlopers, however, were busy with their work at the council today. They would not appear before us. In that case...

I moved my hand, slowly, my fingers tracing a path from her cheek to her soft lips. I leaned in, my fingers still moving slowly across those lips. A normal noble lady's face would be flushed red at this point, should anyone do such a thing. Katarina, however, did not have such a reaction at all — as expected of her.

241

Perhaps she believed that I was removing some dirt from around her lips. Having known her for nine years, I had come to understand her typical thought processes.

As I felt the sensation of her soft lips against my fingers, I wanted a deeper, more personal touch. This desire was welling up in my mind.

"Katarina, you have some dirt on your eyelid. Close your eyes — I shall remove it for you."

"Oh, sure." Without suspecting my words in the slightest, Katarina closed her eyes where she stood. Slowly, I moved my face closer to hers.

"Big Sister! Watch out!" Just as those words were uttered, Katarina was snatched right out of my arms.

Hmph. They always, always do this, interrupting me at such crucial moments... I thought, staring at the culprit responsible for removing Katarina from my side.

As expected, standing before me was Keith, almost out of breath, staring at me with his usual grave expression. It would seem that he had finished his tasks at the council chambers. Wouldn't it have been better if he had taken just a little longer...?

Steadying his breathing as he stood, still staring at me grimly, was Katarina's adopted younger brother, Keith Claes. I had known him for nine years as well. Keith had feelings for Katarina well beyond that of siblings, and he would always make it a point to get in my way. He also had a habit of plotting to cancel the engagement between Katarina and myself, one way or another.

"Ah. If it isn't Keith. Already done with your tasks at the council?" Hiding my irritation, I turned to Keith and smiled in a friendly manner.

"But of course. I was given sufficient motivation to speed up my work thanks to you, Prince Jeord," Keith replied, his face hardening.

And then— "Are you alright, Big Sister?" he asked, staring straight into Katarina's face.

"Hmm? Alright? What do you mean?" Katarina said, still somewhat confused, apparently not understanding what had just happened.

I see that Katarina's tendency to be immeasurably dense is present in full force today. However, I was not entirely pleased with the distance between Katarina and Keith. They were too close — and with that thought in mind, I took her by the arm, pulling her away from him.

Although Keith did not seem to appreciate this development, he did not attempt to yank Katarina back into his arms. The reason for this was simple, really. Keith was simply a late bloomer when it came to Katarina, or perhaps all women. He would never seek to take a relationship to the next level on his own accord.

Despite the fact that he was alluring to the opposite sex and often attracted the gazes of many women, Keith Claes was simply not used to interacting with ladies. Yet even though he was not used to them, Keith still treated women in a most gentlemanly way — and that much was wonderful indeed.

Regardless, he was still an amateur when it came to relationships and love. Perhaps it was due to his own assumptions about how he simply had no luck when it came to love, or perhaps it was because he had been raised together with the immensely dense Katarina.

Even so, the fact that he directed his affections towards Katarina was a most cruel fate. Katarina had, after all, been unwittingly fanning the flames herself without even knowing it. I had lost count of the times I had witnessed Keith's face turn some shade of red, before he quickly distanced himself from his adoptive sister in a panic.

There were times when Keith himself seemed to have noticed how futile that approach was, and also times where he seemed to understand the necessity of moving things forward with his own hands... and yet there he was, his resolve wavering, without me even lifting a finger or saying a single word.

Well, that strange awkwardness of his was something that I could be grateful for, no doubt. After all, Keith and Katarina lived together at Claes Manor, and were essentially together for most of the day. Had Keith not been strangely awkward with romantic relationships in this particular way, I can imagine that something would happen between them.

Honestly, the distance between Katarina and I would have long since been closed, should I have been in Keith's position. As such, I supposed I had to thank Keith for his unique brand of awkwardness.

However, even if that were a good thing, it was most troubling for Keith to keep showing up to interrupt me at crucial moments. If only he had taken just a little longer to get here... Katarina's soft lips would have been mine.

As I stared at her lovely lips with those thoughts crossing my mind, Keith immediately placed himself between us, as if sensing something. He had an alarmed look about him. He was unfortunately very sensitive to such developments — ironic, considering his otherwise awkward nature. He would then stand guard near Katarina, on high alert, as if to prevent me from approaching. How vexing.

But then again, I had already stolen the caress of Katarina's lips once...

It had happened in the previous year, sometime near the onset of winter, when Katarina and the rest of the council found ourselves embroiled in a certain incident.

After Katarina had been confronted and falsely accused by some noble girls in the dining hall, Maria Campbell had gone missing. All of us on the student council searched for her desperately. As the investigation progressed, I arrived at the conclusion that Dark Magic may have been behind this incident in some capacity.

Dark Magic was the terrifying, forbidden power that could manipulate the hearts of others. By my deductions, the target of these events was most likely Katarina. With this in mind, I promptly headed to her side, and soon had her inform me on recent events that had transpired.

Under normal circumstances, this information would only be made known to several high-ranking nobles. One did not simply decide to speak of Dark Magic to others. However, given the danger that Katarina was already in, I made the decision to speak my mind.

While Katarina was merely surprised at first, her face soon paled. She, too, realized the severity of the situation. When she heard that Dark Magic could only be attained by sacrificing the life of another... she began shivering.

It was too alien a world for the gentle and straightforward Katarina to comprehend — or even imagine. I held her tight as her shoulders continued to shake.

The very next morning, Katarina appeared before me, paler than she had been the previous night. I had assumed that she was frightened by what she had heard last night, and had lost sleep because of it. Katarina herself told me that she had witnessed a most terrifying dream.

For reasons unknown to me, she smiled in a peaceful way upon seeing her other friends and myself. We brought the pale Katarina to the infirmary, in hopes of her getting some rest. There, she fell asleep, as if reassured.

Honestly, I had wanted to stay by her side for the entire time. However, I was told by the doctor on duty that she would have trouble falling asleep should I do so. I made my way back to the classrooms after requesting that the doctor inform me once Katarina awoke.

A few hours later, I would direly regret ever having left Katarina's bedside.

It felt as if the very blood in my body froze upon finding her, collapsed, in the academy's courtyard. I ran towards her, panicking. Then an incredible sense of relief washed over me when I realized that she still drew breath.

However, Katarina was now paler than ever. From what we could see, she was simply asleep. Yet no matter how much I called out to her, she simply would not open her eyes.

I exercised all my social influence and power to summon the most well-known doctor in the land, and had him examine Katarina thoroughly. The reason for her slumber, however, remained yet unknown. The situation did not improve.

The possibility of her being in this state because of Dark Magic was relatively high — and with that thought in mind, I had one of the few Wielders of Light in the kingdom brought to me, in hopes of them diagnosing the problem.

I knew that Katarina was in danger… and yet, I was incapable of doing anything to help her. I could not forgive my own weakness. How pathetic.

On the morning of the day after Katarina had fallen into a deep sleep, I paid a visit to her chambers. No response came, no matter how many times I knocked. Upon opening the door, I found that there was only Katarina, still asleep on her bed, and that personal maid of hers by her bedside.

Normally, someone or another would be in her room, but it would seem that no one else was present at the moment. And it would appear that Katarina's personal maid did not notice my entrance — she was most surprised at the sight of me, dropping the cup that she had been holding straight onto the ground. With a resounding shatter, the cup splintered, now mere fragments of broken glass.

"M-My sincere apologies…" Saying so, Katarina's maid knelt down, visibly panicking and upset as she picked up the broken pieces of glass. Her face was white as a sheet, as if she would collapse at any moment.

This particular maid was usually reliable and skilled. She was an exemplar of a maid, and often made any guests who visited Katarina feel at home. She was not the kind of maidservant to break glassware or make mistakes such as this. This was exactly why her panicked expression was painful for me to look at. She, too, admired Katarina greatly — and Katarina, in turn, had deep trust in her maid.

"Have you been feeding her water?" Given that the maid had not even noticed my presence, and the fact that she was holding the cup as I entered, that was most likely to be the case.

"Yes… I thought that… if I give the young miss some water, there might be some changes to her condition… But I have been unable to have her drink very well, thus far…" the maid said, an almost paralyzing look of sadness in her eyes. She then quickly returned to her previous task of gathering up the broken fragments.

After a while, the maid completed her task. I offered to take care of Katarina as she disposed of the fragments. "Please do take care of those fragments. I shall watch over Katarina in your absence."

Although the maid seemed hesitant at first, she eventually bowed her head, and with a murmur of "by your leave," was soon out of the room. And so... Katarina and I were the only ones left in her quarters. Normally, I would have greatly desired such a situation. Now, however... no matter the number of sweet whispers, Katarina would not wake. She did not even react to my touch.

Even so, I approached her bedside, if only so that I could look upon her face.

Katarina was lying perfectly still, hardly drawing breath. This caused me great unease, and I quickly placed my hand onto her lips. Thankfully, she was breathing. I also noticed that her lips were slightly wet — probably due to the efforts of Anne and her feeding cup. There was another cup on the bedside table.

"...*If the young lady continues to sleep, Your Highness... she will be unable to have any water or any food. If this circumstance is prolonged... I fear she will lose her life.*" The doctor's words resurfaced in my mind.

I would not allow this to happen. I lifted the spare cup to my mouth, draining it of its contents. Then, leaning in, I placed my lips against Katarina's, allowing the water to slowly flow into her throat.

To ensure that there would be no leakage of fluids, I sealed Katarina's lips with my own. After a while, I noticed some faint movements in her throat — and then an audible gulp. *She... She drank it! What a relief...* After that, I repeated the exact same motions many times, ensuring that Katarina was well-hydrated.

In the evening of the second day of her slumber, Katarina opened her eyes, apparently having overcome the Dark Magic placed upon her by her own power.

I was desperate at the time — hoping that Katarina would live. While I did not remember the exact sensations I felt then... I could, at the very least, remember that her lips were remarkably soft. Now that I had felt the sensation once, I longed to caress it with my touch once more. However...

"Big Sister, how many times have I told you this? You are not to be alone with Prince Jeord!"

"But... Keith. It's already over! So it's totally fine if Prince Jeord decides to visit me."

"What...? What is over? Totally fine...? I'm afraid I do not understand, Big Sister..."

With this, it did not seem like another opportunity would present itself anytime soon. *If I had known this would happen, I would have been more... forward, on the previous occasion.* Those were the thoughts in my mind as I observed Katarina and Keith, neither one seemingly able to understand the other.

"Lady Katarina... are you safe?"

Yet another individual to stand in my way, I see. This one was out of breath as well.

"Oh! If it isn't Mary. Hmm… everyone seems somewhat early today. But… what do you mean by 'safe'…?"

"Ah, yes. You see, Lady Katarina… there were some… incidents today. I am glad that you are safe, however." Saying so, she turned to me, smiling ever so faintly. This woman was none other than Lady Mary Hunt — my brother's fiancée.

Theoretically, she was my twin brother Alan Stuart's fiancée. Mary herself, however, did not seem to view Alan that way. She only had eyes for Katarina, and seemed to always be chasing after her. Although she was quite a beautiful girl at a glance, her inner personality was something much akin to mine. How long has it been since I had noticed this…? Mary was even more troublesome than Keith, with her methods intensifying by the day. She was a most fearsome enemy.

"H-Hey! Where are you running off to, Mary?" Standing behind Mary was none other than my brother, Alan. In truth, Alan, too, had been drawn towards Katarina. He'd had feelings for her for almost eight years now. However, thanks to his relatively thick mind, haughty tendency, and the schemes of his fiancée, Mary Hunt, Alan had yet to notice these feelings himself. Truly, a man to be pitied.

However, even my dense brother seemed to have awakened to his own feelings following the Dark Magic incident. His attitude to Katarina had changed somewhat. Even so, I had let my guard down — Alan was not the kind to lay his hands on his brother's fiancée just because of how he felt.

However… Mary Hunt, his very own fiancée and strategist, had apparently utilized him in one of her plans. As we were brothers, Alan's quarters were adjacent to mine. Alan had apparently been instructed to report my movements to Mary… and so he had become an unexpectedly troublesome foe.

Alan aside, the fact that Mary's methods became more and more intense by the day was troubling indeed. In fact, I was now more aware of Alan becoming closer to Mary after becoming aware of his feelings. *Is this some sort of camaraderie? He has his own fiancée, does he not? I would greatly prefer that Alan and Miss Hunt get along well and keep to themselves. More importantly, they should stop interrupting the quality time I spend with Katarina.*

While this small field supposedly only belonged to Katarina and myself, before I knew it, the entire student council was here. Although I had put my mind to it and finished my work early, I supposed I could not discount their capabilities either.

In the end, Sophia Ascart and Maria Campbell also arrived on the scene, and the small field soon became quite the hive of activity.

"Even so, Prince Jeord... the speed at which you work, and the fact that you can handle any kind of documentation, is most impressive."

"It is nothing special. Today was simply a fluke."

Maria, who had apparently been surprised at the speed of my work, offered me some compliments. I, however, responded in a relatively vague manner. Although the other members of the council had deduced the reason for me rushing through my work, and had ambivalent expressions about them as they did so, Maria had not seemed to notice this.

This young girl, Maria Campbell — a commoner and a Wielder of Light, had a good head on her shoulders. At the same time, however, she did slip up from time to time. As such, she sometimes did do very strange things indeed, although not to the extent that Katarina would.

In fact, if I had not met Katarina... given how I was, I would have found her most interesting. Even now, Maria continued to work hard, and gave her all in everything she did. *Yes... I think I would have been very fond of her indeed. However...*

"Ah, right. Lady Katarina... I made some treats for you today, too. Please do try some, if you would like." Saying so, Maria presented a box of baked goods in Katarina's general direction. Almost immediately. Katarina happily bounded to her side.

"Thank you so much, Maria! Oh, I love you so!" Katarina's face was already full of unbridled adoration.

Yes... Maria Campbell. I did think of her as someone I could have become fond of, or so I thought. However, she was far too close to my fiancée. It would be quite a problem if Katarina grew overly fond of this girl. In fact, Katarina was already more or less thoroughly domesticated by Maria's baked goods. It was clear that she liked this girl very much indeed.

To make things worse, Katarina, who was already enough of a natural charmer herself, had long since succeeded in making Maria fall for her. Sometimes I would see the two of them together, almost looking like were actual lovers. *Ah, what a terrifying sight.*

As such, the very existence of Maria herself meant that she was an enemy as well, hellbent on getting between Katarina and myself. If I had to say, Maria was different from the rest — she was a powerful foe, almost from another dimension.

As I looked upon Katarina, who was currently happily munching away on Maria's homemade treats at a small table in the corner of the crop field, I felt a somewhat complicated mix of emotions rise up from within me. And then...

"Ah! Big Brother, this way, please!" Sophia Ascart's voice.

I followed the direction of her voice with my eyes. As expected, standing there was Sophia's brother, Nicol Ascart, who had graduated from the academy in the previous year. Accompanying them was the individual who, up until the middle of last year, was the student council president — Raphael Wolt.

"Well met, Prince Jeord. It has been a while." The owner of that voice was none other than Nicol himself. Famous for his charms, it was said that his beauty captivated both man and woman alike. I returned his greeting, and inquired about his presence on the academy grounds.

"I have business with the Magical Ministry's research facility on the campus today," Nicol replied with his usual expressionless face.

Raphael, who was accompanying them, was also currently working at that particular research building. He had been working there today as well, when Nicol, who had been visiting, apparently called out to him. He was then invited along... which explains his presence.

"Ah! Master Nicol, Raphael! It's been a while, hasn't it?" Apparently Katarina, who had been stuffing her face with food all this while, finally noticed the presence of Nicol and Raphael.

"Katarina. I am glad you are well," Nicol said, his previously stoic expression melting away into an alluring smile.

Ah, yes. Of course. This Nicol, too, has feelings for Katarina. Even so, Nicol was quite the respectable man, and had a good amount of common sense about him. He would not think of lusting after someone else's fiancée. After all, he had been strangely blessed with a mysterious, yet troublesome charm.

If anything, it seemed like Nicol's charm only increased as the years went by. Even Katarina, whose tendency to be dense likely ranked somewhere near the top of this kingdom, had recently started to become attracted to his smile. Not exactly a development I could be relaxed about... And then.

"Big Brother, let us try some of Lady Maria's treats, too! This way..." I had not even noticed her movements, but there she was. Sophia Ascart, already seated next to Katarina, was calling out to Nicol.

Nicol's younger sister, Sophia, admired Katarina greatly as well. In fact, seeing her brother take Katarina's hand in marriage was apparently an ambition of hers — Sophia the matchmaker, so to speak. Although she was originally a quiet, withdrawn girl, the long years she had spent with Katarina and Mary were perhaps responsible for her transformation into a bold girl. She seemed completely different from the shirking creature that I had met in my childhood.

In addition, Raphael, who had accompanied the two of them here, was also gazing at Katarina lovingly. Raphael's circumstances were somewhat complex to begin with — and although he did not initially show any sign of emotion for Katarina, that all changed after the incident. It did not take me long to find him staring at Katarina with passionate gazes after he returned to the campus.

Honestly... Katarina Claes. Just how many people do you intend to charm with your wiles...? I inwardly sighed as I continued observing Katarina, who was currently still stuffing her face.

She was silly, naive, and dense... a noble lady that was most unlike her peers — that was Katarina. Even so, she would mysteriously draw other people to her. Those with loneliness or sadness in their hearts often found themselves drawn to her earnest personality.

To those who lived in the world of politics and conspiracy that were the noble circles of these lands, or to those who desperately tried to read the intents and charades of others, Katarina's straightforward gaze must resemble the warm rays of the sun enveloping their hearts. This was why so many were drawn to the girl known as Katarina Claes, and found their lives changed because of their interactions with her.

With all that being said, Katarina was simply a little too much of a charmer. I had far too many enemies on the field. *However... I suppose this is alright.* Her inflated cheeks as she enjoyed snacks with her friends was quite the hilarious sight. Perhaps it was fine for things to stay like this for a while — maybe even I had been significantly influenced by Katarina, to think of things in such a way.

I had been looking at Katarina all this time — and then... her aqua-blue eyes met mine.

"Would you like to try some too, Prince Jeord?" It would seem that Katarina had associated my gaze with a desire for the food she was currently having. She reached into the small basket of treats and took one, raising it up and offering it to me.

"Hmm. Very well then. I shall have one." I leaned in towards Katarina, closing my lips around the snack — and her finger. "Most delicious," I said with a slight smile. Almost immediately, I could feel a series of intense gazes dig into my being.

Katarina herself, however... did not seem to understand what just happened, as that absent-minded look was still on her face. "Ah... Prince Jeord. You didn't finish it all! There's still some here."

Keith, however, soon leapt into action, his expression darker than anything I had ever seen before. "Big Sister, quickly, your finger!" he exclaimed, grabbing Katarina's arm, and then the finger that had met my lips just moments ago. He fervently cleaned it with a handkerchief.

"Ah! Wh-What is it, Keith? That hurts a little!" It would seem that Keith had rubbed her finger just a little too hard. Katarina's voice soon rose in protest.

"Keith. Do be careful — you seem to be hurting Katarina."

"B-But that's because of you!" Keith snapped back.

"Exactly! Prince Jeord, whatever were you thinking?" Sophia added.

"...Unbelievable. How dirty of you!" Mary exclaimed.

"Serious! What've you done..." Alan grumbled.

With those exclamations, members of the previous and current student council soon placed themselves between Katarina and I, forcibly separating us.

Ah, well. I suppose I do like Katarina's smile as she laughs and plays with her friends like this. Perhaps it would be alright for this situation to last just a little longer... However, I have absolutely no intention of handing Katarina over to anyone.

I flashed the still-stunned Katarina a brief smile. *Now, then... how should I go about obtaining some quality time for the two of us next...?*

Hello. It is Satoru Yamaguchi. Thank you very much for purchasing this book. It is because of the readers, and the support that I have received from everyone, that I was able to publish this book two months after the first. Everyone, thank you very much for your support.

In this second book, Katarina entered the Academy of Magic — the stage on which the scenario of *Fortune Lover* plays out. The original protagonist of *Fortune Lover* finally makes her appearance too. I hope that you find her to your liking.

I would also like to thank Nami Hidaka-sama, who has provided the illustrations for this volume as well. The rival characters and love interests, who are now splendidly grown up, were portrayed magnificently. Specifically Maria, who was the original protagonist of *Fortune Lover*, was drawn so lovably. I was impressed, and couldn't help but think, "Yes, she is just how the protagonist of an otome game would look!"

Lastly, I would like to thank the editor in chief, who has provided me with so much advice over these months. I would also like to thank all those who have assisted me in the publishing process. I am deeply grateful, from the bottom of my heart.

Everyone, thank you very much.

Satoru Yamaguchi

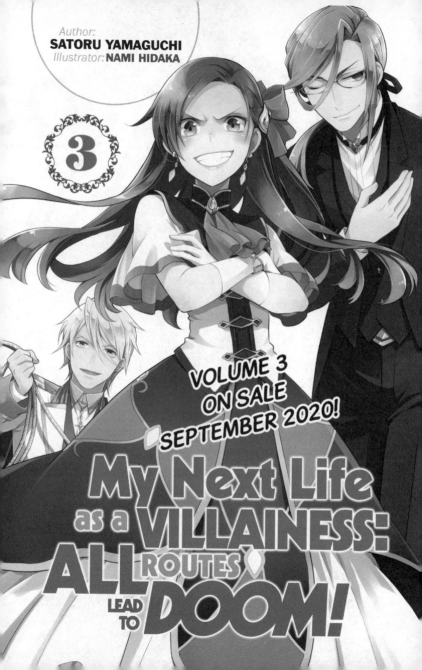

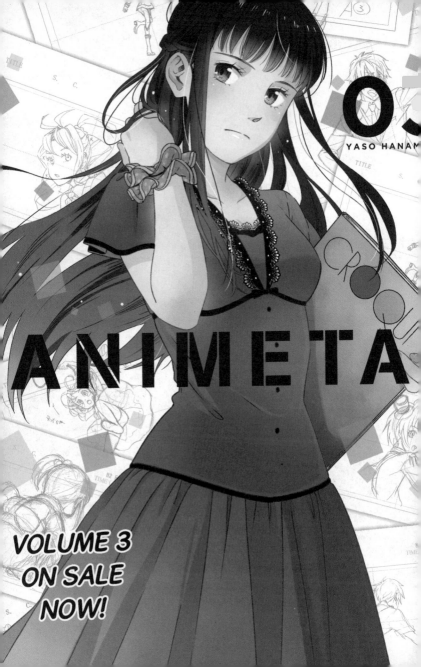

ASCENDAN
OF A
BOOKWOR
I'll do anything t
become a librari
Part 2 Apprentice Shr
Maiden Vol. 3
Author: **Miya Kazuki**
Illustrator: **You Shiina**

NOVEL:
PART 2 VOL. 3
ON SALE
OCTOBER 2020!

MANGA:
PART 1 VOL. 1
ON SALE
SEPTEMBER 202

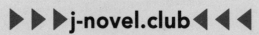

J-Novel Club Lineup

Ebook Releases Series List

Altina the Sword Princess
An Archdemon's Dilemma:
    How to Love Your Elf Bride
Arifureta Zero
Arifureta: From Commonplace
    to World's Strongest
Ascendance of a Bookworm
Beatless
Bibliophile Princess
By the Grace of the Gods
Campfire Cooking in Another World
    with My Absurd Skill
Can Someone Please Explain What's
    Going On?!
The Combat Baker and Automaton Waitress
Cooking with Wild Game
Crest of the Stars
Demon King Daimaou
Demon Lord, Retry!
Der Werwolf: The Annals of Veight
The Economics of Prophecy
The Faraway Paladin
Full Metal Panic!
The Greatest Magicmaster's Retirement Plan
Grimgar of Fantasy and Ash
Her Majesty's Swarm
The Holy Knight's Dark Road
How a Realist Hero Rebuilt the Kingdom
How NOT to Summon a Demon Lord
I Refuse to Be Your Enemy!
I Saved Too Many Girls and Caused the
    Apocalypse
I Shall Survive Using Potions!
If It's for My Daughter, I'd Even Defeat a
    Demon Lord
In Another World With My Smartphone
Infinite Dendrogram
Infinite Stratos
Invaders of the Rokujouma!?
Isekai Rebuilding Project
JK Haru is a Sex Worker in Another World
Kobold King
Kokoro Connect
Last and First Idol
Lazy Dungeon Master
The Magic in this Other World is
    Too Far Behind!
The Master of Ragnarok & Blesser of Einherjar
Middle-Aged Businessman, Arise in Another
    World!
Mixed Bathing in Another Dimension

My Next Life as a Villainess: All Routes Lead
    to Doom!
Otherside Picnic
Outbreak Company
Outer Ragna
Record of Wortenia War
Seirei Gensouki: Spirit Chronicles
Seriously Seeking Sister! Ultimate Vampire
    Princess Just Wants Little Sister; Plenty of
    Service Will Be Provided!
Sexiled: My Sexist Party Leader Kicked
    Me Out, So I Teamed Up With a Mythical
    Sorceress!
Sorcerous Stabber Orphen:
    The Wayward Journey
The Tales of Marielle Clarac
Tearmoon Empire
Teogonia
There Was No Secret Evil-Fighting
    Organization (srsly?!), So I Made One
    MYSELF!
The Underdog of the Eight Greater Tribes
The Unwanted Undead Adventurer
Welcome to Japan, Ms. Elf!
The White Cat's Revenge as Plotted from the
    Dragon King's Lap
The World's Least Interesting Master
    Swordsman

Manga Series:
A Very Fairy Apartment
An Archdemon's Dilemma:
    How to Love Your Elf Bride
Animeta!
Ascendance of a Bookworm
Cooking with Wild Game
Demon Lord, Retry!
Discommunication
The Faraway Paladin
How a Realist Hero Rebuilt the Kingdom
I Shall Survive Using Potions!
Infinite Dendrogram
The Magic in this Other World is
    Too Far Behind!
Marginal Operation
The Master of Ragnarok & Blesser of Einherjar
Seirei Gensouki: Spirit Chronicles
Sorcerous Stabber Orphen:
    The Reckless Journey
Sweet Reincarnation
The Unwanted Undead Adventurer